D0550516

# CELEBRATING ONE WORLD

# CELEBRATING ONE WORLD

A worship resource on social justice

*Edited by Linda Jones and Annabel Shilson-Thomas*
*Music compiled by Bernadette Farrell*

HarperCollins*Publishers*

HarperCollins*Religious*
Part of HarperCollins*Publishers*
77-85 Fulham Palace Road, London W6 8JB

First published in Great Britain in 1998 by HarperCollins*Religious*

10 9 8 7 6 5 4 3 2 1

Copyright © 1998 CAFOD

Linda Jones, Annabel Shilson-Thomas and Bernadette Farrell assert the moral right to be identified as the compilers of this work

A catalogue record for this book is available from the British Library

ISBN 0 00 599376 8

Text illustrations by Josephine Sumner

Printed and bound in Great Britain by Mackays of Chatham plc

CONDITIONS OF SALE
This book is sold subject to the condition that it shall not, by way of trade or otherwise, be lent, re-sold, hired out or otherwise circulated without the publisher's prior consent in any form of binding or cover other than that in which it is published and without a similar condition including this condition being imposed on the subsequent purchaser.

All rights reserved. No part of this publication may be reproduced, stored in a retrieval system, or transmitted, in any form or by any means, electronic, mechanical, photocopying, recording or otherwise, without the prior permission of the publishers.

*With thanks to Sister Una McCreesh for her research.*

## About CAFOD

CAFOD is one of the UK's major overseas aid agencies and is the official relief and development agency of the Catholic Church in England and Wales. It works through partner organizations overseas supporting people in need, whatever their race or religion. As well as funding over 1,000 projects in 75 of the world's poorest countries, it responds to emergency situations worldwide. In this country, it campaigns on social justice, helping people make connections between their lives and the lives of people in the Third World. It aims to be as cost-effective as possible, spending on average less than ten pence in the pound on fund raising and administration.

## About the editors

Linda Jones works in the Public Education section of CAFOD as Senior Campaign Coordinator. Before joining CAFOD in 1991 she taught in both secondary schools and adult education. Her main interests are music, liturgy and popular education in Latin America, and she has spent time living and working in Chile. Whilst with CAFOD she has also visited Nicaragua, Zimbabwe and Kenya. She is studying for an MA in religion and education, with a particular focus on liturgy and social justice.

Annabel Shilson-Thomas works for CAFOD as a writer and editor. She has travelled widely in the developing world and has spent time living and working in the Middle East. She has worked in publishing for a number of years and has written several children's books including *A First Puffin Picture Book of Bible Stories* and *Stories from World Religions*, both published by Penguin Children's Books. Her interest in liturgy was fostered while studying for a degree in Theology and through her work as an Anglican curate in south-east London. She is married to an Anglican priest and they have a one-year-old son, Aidan.

Bernadette Farrell is currently a consultant liturgist and musician for the Diocese of Westminster. She has worked in the East End of London for ten years, actively involved with people of many faiths and cultures. At the forefront of liturgical renewal in the Roman Catholic Church, Bernadette is well-known as a composer and text writer. She has travelled extensively giving workshops and now lives in London with her husband Owen Alstott and their daughter Jo.

# CONTENTS

# PREFACE

The material which has been collected to make this book comes from around the world. Despite the diversity of its origins, it is held together by a common thread: the search for social justice. This is not a new concern. The exploitation of the poor by the rich is an age-old problem. What has changed is its sheer scale and complexity. The poverty of the poor South seems so far removed from the affluence of the rich North that it is difficult to connect the two. We may ask how the lives of refugees in the Congo, factory workers in Bangladesh, and landless peasants in Brazil have anything to do with us. But they will ask a different question: 'Will you listen to our story – how colonialism raped our countries, leaving behind unworkable national boundaries and massive national debts; how your demand for cheap goods leads to virtual slavery in our factories; how the creation of a land-owning elite means we now have nowhere to grow food for our families?'

And what is our response? As Christians we need to have ears that hear, for the poor of the world are today's prophets, challenging us to be good neighbours, to work for justice and the establishment of God's kingdom, where all are valued and none exploited. They remind us that we cannot be in a right relationship with God if we are out of step with our neighbours and disconnected from our world.

This need for balance, harmony and restoration is at the very heart of creation. The seventh day is a time for rest, not only for God, but for all humankind. The centrality of restoring creation, of making all things new, underpins all calls for justice, past and present. The Old Testament prophets constantly call their hearers back to the Exodus, to the Israelites' release from slavery and restoration as a people. It is this that charges the people of Israel with responsibility for those on the margins. Their own spiritual restoration through fasting and sacrifices is a delusion if the physical restoration of the poor and hungry is neglected.

> Is not this the fast I require:
> to loose the fetters of injustice,
> to untie the knots of the yoke,
> and set free those who are oppressed,
> tearing off every yoke?
> Is it not sharing your food with the hungry,
> taking the homeless poor into your house,
> clothing the naked when you meet them,
> and never evading a duty to your kinsfolk?

*Isaiah 58:6–7*

Developing this prophetic call for justice, Jesus constantly calls people to turn around, to make reparation for past wrongs and to start afresh. And so Zaccheus pays back more than he had extorted and turns to follow Jesus, the man from the margins, who came to bring good news to the poor, freedom to the oppressed and sight to the blind (Luke 4:18–19).

Likewise, Christ continues to call us from death to life. As the parable of the sheep and the goats indicates, our own restoration and calling is bound up with the restoration of the poor. We might well ask, ' "Lord, when was it that we saw you hungry and fed you, or thirsty and gave you drink, a stranger and took you home, or naked and clothed you? When did we see you ill or in prison, and come to visit you?" And the king will answer, "Truly I tell you: anything you did for one of my brothers and sisters here, however insignificant, you did for me" ' (Matthew 25:37–40).

Today, we continue to meet Christ in the homeless and destitute, the refugee and the asylum seeker, the bonded labourer and the child worker. Until there is justice for them, there can be no peace for us and no peace for our world. Through them Christ challenges us to change and be changed. The choices which we make and the actions that we take – from the coffee that we drink to the shoes that we wear – are bound up with the healing and restoration of the whole of creation. Christ invites us to engage actively in God's struggle and to make it ours. We are called to be his disciples, to be good news to the poor. Just as Jesus went out from the synagogue in Nazareth to begin his mission, we too are called to go out from the Church and into the world, to listen and to respond.

It is hoped that the material which has been collected in this book will be one small step along the way. Its purpose is to help us to make connections between our lives and our faith, so that our worship is outward looking, both reflecting our mission and inspiring us to journey on in the company of our brothers and sisters in the South. Like those who have gone before us, we are a pilgrim people.

*Annabel Shilson-Thomas*

# SOME HINTS ON CREATING LITURGIES

*Planning a liturgy*

The liturgy – the form of service which public worship takes – reflects our values and visions and expresses our belief about God. This is conveyed not just through the spoken word, but through a variety of media – music, art, smell, even taste and touch. At best, a liturgy engages all our senses, recharges our spiritual batteries and sends us out into the world, refreshed and ready to serve.

In order to do this, the liturgy's design needs to have shape and movement and its content needs to have clarity and vision. This may sound daunting, but don't be put off. The key is not so much divine inspiration as forward planning, careful preparation and shared creativity. Working in groups not only shares the load, but provides an ideal forum for the interchange of ideas.

GETTING STARTED
In the early stages of planning, it may be helpful to bear in mind the following key questions:

1. Are we working within the parameters of a set service (e.g. the Mass), or are we creating an alternative liturgy?
2. What liturgical season are we in?
3. Will the liturgy fall on a fast or feast day?
4. What is its theme?
5. Who is the liturgy for? Adults, children, all-age?

6.  How long will it last?
7.  What is its message?
8.  How can we make the best use of the available worship space?
9.  What musical resources are available?
10. How much preparation time is there?

WRITING A SKELETON PLAN

If you are working within the boundaries of a set liturgy, the bare bones of the service will already be there. If creating your own liturgy, the next stage of planning is to write a skeleton service (keeping the above questions in mind), upon which hymns, readings, prayers and so forth can be hung. For example:

1.  Call to worship.
2.  Hymn/music.
3.  Prayer of confession.
4.  Reading.
5.  Hymn/music.
6.  Talk/Drama.
7.  Silence/time for reflection.
8.  Symbolic action.
9.  Prayers.
10. Musical piece.
11. Hymn.
12. Dismissal.

At this point, check the service for movement, balance and variety, and be careful not to overload it. Too many items or too many words may cause indigestion! As far as you are able, estimate how long each item will last, and, within the structure, leave room for silence and reflection.

CHOOSING THE READINGS AND MUSIC

When choosing the music (hymns, chants, etc.), make sure that it reflects the theme and mood of the liturgy and serves the right purpose. For example, the first hymn usually acts as a call to worship, so the words and music need to reflect this, whereas a hymn at the end of the service usually acts as a dismissal, so its purpose is to send us out into the world.

Readings (biblical, poems or prose) are the most obvious means of articulating the theme of the liturgy, so pick them well. If choosing a biblical reading, look at different translations before deciding which one to use. Ask yourself questions such as, 'Does it read well out loud? Is the language inclusive? Is it suitable for children?' and then decide.

## LEADING THE WORSHIP

Bear in mind that what a congregation sees helps to form their ideas about God and informs their faith. If we believe in a God who values people irrespective of their gender, sexuality, race, colour or ability, then as far as possible, those involved in leading the worship need to reflect this diversity. Sometimes, making worship visibly inclusive means allowing extra time to train and rehearse people who would not normally take a lead. But avoid tokenism. Rota people in and be open to new talent.

## PRACTICE AND REHEARSING

It is worthwhile for worship leaders to walk through an unfamiliar liturgy beforehand to check for any unforeseen hitches. Readers need to be rehearsed – watch out for speed and audibility – and music needs to be practised. Where unfamiliar hymns or tunes are to be used, a run-through with the congregation before the service or at some other time makes for better worship.

## PRODUCING AN ORDER OF SERVICE

Where possible, a simple order of service, which is clear and easy to read and with good directions, will help worshippers to relax into the service. Having to juggle several books and pieces of paper can be very off-putting to the uninitiated.

Look at the size and shape of the worship space, and decide how best to use it. If the service is to be held in a conventional church setting, try to use the space creatively. Use light and dark to best effect. Arrange flowers or other displays to complement your theme. Arrange the pews or chairs in a way that brings the congregation together, and make imaginative use of symbols (see the next section). In a less conventional setting, you can experiment more easily. Perhaps you could dispense with seating altogether and create your own focal point for the liturgy. The possibilities are there to be realized. Take a few risks and see how they work.

## Using symbols

Symbols – objects, actions or words which represent, recall or communicate a reality larger than ourselves – are used in worship to express our feelings and beliefs about God. At the same time, they help to focus our thoughts and create atmosphere.

### EVERYDAY SYMBOLS
The most obvious example of a Christian symbol is the cross, which recalls the crucifixion and reminds us of God's gift of salvation. Many other symbols are less specific. Their richness lies in the fact that they are everyday objects with a multitude of associations; for example, bread, wine, water and light. To them is attached an abundance of meaning. The bread and wine remind us of food (spiritual and physical), work, celebration, sacrifice and so on. Water, as the baptism service reminds us, is associated both with life (i.e. refreshment and liberation) and death (i.e. the deep waters of destruction). Light, too, is rich in meaning, for its presence brings truth, warmth, growth and health.

## SYMBOLIC ACTION

Symbols are not only helpful as visual aids, but can also be used in symbolic actions. For example, lighting a votive candle as we intercede keeps the prayer 'burning'; laying down a stone as we ask God for help or forgiveness allows us to let go of the burden we are carrying; placing a flower in a vase as we pray can be an expression of thanksgiving, and so on.

Sometimes an object can be used to help us get in touch with a particular experience. For example, a bowl of sand can symbolize the desert and can be used to recall the Israelites' wilderness experience, or the temptations of Jesus. In the same way, it can also put us in touch with our own internal wanderings and can help us to focus on our spiritual journey. So long as a symbol has appropriate meaning and aids worship, use it.

## SYMBOLIC MOVEMENT

We tend to associate churches with stillness and services with sitting still. While stillness has an important part to play in worship, so has movement. A procession can be used to symbolize a journey, spiritual or otherwise. Different attitudes of prayer – bowing, kneeling, prostrating – can symbolize our inner attitudes towards God, while for the more adventurous, mime and dance can often convey what words cannot express.

## USING OUR SENSES TO EXPRESS THE SYMBOLIC

Very often we limit the way we worship by only engaging two of our senses – sight and hearing. By employing all our senses we engage our whole selves in worship. For example, the smell of incense reminds us of God's pervasive presence; the scent of flowers makes us think of the richness of God's creation; the aroma of freshly baked bread reminds us of Christ, the bread of life.

Our sense of touch can be employed in symbolic actions, too. For example, sharing the peace symbolizes our oneness as a body; standing with arms outstretched expresses our openness to God. Less obvious ways of using touch are no less effective. For example, handling a nail can be a useful aid to help us meditate on the crucifixion, or feeling a stone can remind us of our hardness of heart.

Even our sense of taste can contribute to a better understanding of our faith: bitter herbs, such as horseradish, can remind us of the bitterness of the wilderness experience; honey can remind us of the 'sweetness' of God's word; while an Agape (a shared meal in the manner of the early Christians) can symbolize solidarity, togetherness and celebration.

Be open to symbols and use them well.

## How to use music

Each section in this book has a selection of songs which reflects its theme. Some are already well known, others may be new to you. Whether 'new' or 'old', music has an important part to play in the liturgy. It is integral to worship and carries enormous power.

Music is creative. It can build an atmosphere of celebration, of stillness and reflection, of questioning and commitment. Music is participative. People can sing, clap, play instruments, read words over music, hum the chorus, dance or meditate. Music reaches people; it moves them and it makes them move.

To leave the choice of music until the last minute – a quick flick through the hymn book to find something everybody knows – is a lost opportunity. Music is central to the liturgy and cannot be an add-on. It needs to be included in the initial stages of all liturgical thinking and planning.

So first check whether the day of the service is a feast day or a day set aside for special prayers, say for peace or homelessness. Then look at the biblical readings and choose your songs and music to reflect their message, as well as making sure they fit the different parts of the service. If possible, plan together with the priest or whoever is leading the service. Make sure they know which parts of the service they are expected to sing, and which parts of the service will be led by the choir or musicians. There is little that is more frustrating than practising a sung response all week, only to find the leader of the service launching into a spoken version!

You do not need to be an expert to make music. Invite others to help. It is usually possible to find at least one instrumentalist. They do not have to be an organist or a pianist. You could try a single guitar or a recorder, or ask someone with a strong, clear voice which they can keep in tune (!) to lead. If none of this is possible, then use a tape player. For example, people can sing together with a Taizé chant on tape, or they can listen to taped music as an aid to meditation.

Think, too, about the balance of instruments you use. Some songs need trumpets and drums, others need a flute and guitar. Not everyone has to play for every hymn. Children learning to play should be encouraged and welcomed. If they make more mistakes than the more experienced players, so what? Music should be inclusive. It should be as good as possible, but it does not have to be perfect every time. This does not mean that it should be done carelessly. A carefully built up atmosphere of prayer and calm can be destroyed in ten seconds by someone knocking over a music stand, twanging a guitar string or whispering, 'What are we playing next?'

If you already have a choir and/or an instrumental group in your parish or community, you have a wonderful opportunity. But you also have a built-in danger. Many congregations heave a collective, if subconscious, sigh of relief at the sight of a choir. They feel that it lets them off the hook – they don't have to join in. The role of a choir is to switch people on to music so that they feel inspired to join in – not to switch them off!

A good cantor can be a wonderful asset, too. She or he can lead the singing, sing the difficult bits in between the choruses and inspire the congregation. However, some get carried away and think they're on the West End stage in a starring role! This should be gently discouraged, as no one else will join in. Perhaps such a person should be pointed in the direction of a training course. Training for cantors and choir leaders is available in many dioceses and church organizations.

Encourage the congregation. Teach them anything which is new before the service – but introduce only one new piece at a time, and use it at regular intervals over a period of weeks (not every week, of course!) so that it is not forgotten. Praise their efforts – but don't patronize them. The chances are that someone told them years ago that they were useless at singing and sounded like a drowning cat! You have to undo the damage.

Music is a great responsibility, but it is also fun. In one way or another everybody can join in and feel part of something special. Good music *is* worship.

## Designing a school assembly

The key to an effective school assembly – one that engages the pupils and moves them on – is preparation. Decide well in advance when and where the assembly will take place. Ensure that the venue is booked and check that no one else is using it directly before or after you. Notify the staff and request that any school notices should be dealt with at the beginning of the assembly and kept to a minimum. Giving priority to the assembly is important.

Plenty of time and thought needs to be given to the structure, content and presentation. An assembly that is well thought out, well rehearsed, and which carries a pertinent message will hold the young people's attention and provide them with food for thought. At best it will awaken a pupil's spirituality by tapping into the heart of issues relevant to his or her world and relating them to a wider social and spiritual context. Often a subject which the pupils have been studying – for example, environmental issues, human geography, climatic changes, health care, food technology and so on – will suggest an assembly theme. Sometimes local issues will provide a focus: for example, the closing down of a refugee hostel or the start of a homelessness project.

When working with children, enough time has to be built into the schedule of preparation to allow them time not only to develop their ideas, but to experiment with their execution and to build up enough confidence to produce results. Pupils need to feel involved from the start, so that they can own the finished product and take pride in their work. To cut back on preparation time will lead to an assembly that is staff born rather than pupil led. The consequent result will be lack of pupil attention.

If a large number of pupils are involved (for example, if a class is taking an assembly), it may be helpful to set up small working groups to take responsibility for different parts of the assembly. Each group would need to be well briefed and to know the parameters within which they were working. It may be that an initial working party will need to map out the shape and form of the assembly, ensuring that it has balance and variety. The remit of other working parties might be as follows: music, prayers, dance, setting up the worship area, and so on.

While pupils need to feel free to develop their own ideas, they will almost certainly appreciate some help and encouragement along the way. As far as possible, ensure that there are adequate resources available and people who can point them in the right direction – for example, the staff of the RE, Music and Drama departments, as well as interested individual teachers and school chaplains.

If the assembly has a development angle, bringing in help from outside the school is often valuable. Development agencies are always happy to provide information and material (many have their own schools department), and sometimes guest speakers. Use any contacts which the pupils and staff may have with people or organizations linked to the developing world.

Before rehearsals begin, make sure that everything hangs together and that the overall message is clear and focused. Check that the assembly is not overloaded and that there is time for reflection. A clear beginning and a clear end – perhaps marked with a communal prayer to help people move in and out of worship – is essential, as is a level of humour to lighten potentially heavy subjects.

Practice is important. Readers need to be rehearsed, singers heard, musicians taken through their music, and so on. Try to use people's talents imaginatively. Everyone will have something to offer. Ask someone to watch the rehearsals, to offer constructive criticism and to time everything – a paragraph takes much longer to read out than one might think! Preferably, spoken parts should be either very simple or so well rehearsed that a script is not needed.

Before the assembly itself, allow time for quiet. A sense of the occasion – an act of worship – needs to be realized. Those leading the assembly need to feel confident and relaxed, not fraught and anxious. Afterwards they may need time to debrief. A post-mortem is always valuable to assess what things worked and what could have been done better.

If feeling daunted, remember that there is no substitute for advance preparation, pupil involvement and plenty of practice. Assemblies are hard work – but they are worth it!

## Working with youth groups

Young people are full of energy, creativity and enthusiasm. They have gifts that need to be tapped and ideas that need to be explored. They are an exciting group of people to work with, and, like any other group, they need to feel valued and listened to.

The key to successfully devising a liturgy with young people is involvement. Ask them to choose a theme relevant to their world. It may be connected to a piece of work or related to the liturgical year. If they are taking responsibility for elements within a set liturgy – for example, the Mass – the boundaries, although flexible, are already set. If creating an alternative liturgy, work with them to devise a framework. This gives them clear boundaries to guide their thinking, as well as freedom to develop their own ideas. Such a framework may look something like this:

1. Music
2. Opening prayer
3. Reading
4. Drama
5. Reflection
6. Music
7. Symbolic action
8. Intercessions
9. Music
10. Closing prayer

Encourage the young people to write their own prayers, choose their own readings (biblical and non-biblical), devise their own drama or dance routine, pick their own music (contemporary as well as more traditional hymns and songs) and think up a symbolic action which reflects the theme of the liturgy.

Within a large group, there are usually people who have particular gifts and leanings. It may well be that they wish to work on some areas of the liturgy rather than others. If that is the case, divide the group up and ask each sub-group to take responsibility for different elements of the service – for example, music or drama.

Many young people enjoy drama and see it as a medium through which to express their own understanding and perception of a subject. Others may feel more secure with something more structured – a dramatized reading, perhaps. Don't be too prescriptive. Allow for experimentation and perhaps a degree of failure!

Music – at the heart of youth culture today – is very important. Contemporary music is likely to hold more meaning for young people than more traditional church music and can be used to great effect in alternative liturgies. The words and lyrics often express questions which we all grapple with, as well as addressing some of the struggles particularly pertinent to growing up.

Those who play instruments can help in preparing the music, but also try to involve the less well trained. Percussion instruments are ideal for introducing the uninitiated to the joys of playing together and can add life and vitality to a liturgy.

Singing, too, will need to be practised, whether solo, in groups or all together. Sung responses to prayer and Taizé-style chants are always popular. They also add atmosphere and are easy to pick up. Sometimes singing can form the background to a meditation. However, don't make the mistake of filling every available space with sound. Like any other group, young people need and appreciate silence, in which to muse, reflect and pray. Silence in itself is creative and should be built into the liturgy.

Many young people enjoy arts and crafts and will readily employ their talents to create wall hangings and liturgical symbols. For example, a papier mâché globe with a slit in the top becomes a symbol of solidarity when used as a focus of prayer during the liturgy: as people pray they drop their petition through the slit in the globe, expressing solidarity with their Third World neighbours. A life map made from newspaper cuttings and magazine pictures illustrating the lives of people overseas is another tool that can aid prayer. An alternative to a life map could be a Salvadorian cross – one that tells a story through pictures. Murals and home-made altar cloths, collages and home-made hunger cloths are also popular. On a less elaborate scale, everyday objects such as bread, water, wine and seeds can be used imaginatively and to great effect. For example, the planting of seeds – symbols of new life – can be used to symbolize hope; washing one another's feet can symbolize service, and so on.

Young people will always be full of ideas. Your job is to encourage them, to ensure that no one is left out, and that enough practice time is built into the preparation. Good luck!

# HOW TO USE THIS BOOK

The layout of this book is designed for easy access. The
material is grouped under eight themes: Environment and
Land; Basic Needs; The Excluded; Conflict, War and Peace;
Work and Debt; Women; Solidarity; and Celebrating Hope.
Each section contains prayers, poems, readings, biblical
quotations, hymns and songs, and each item is numbered.
Hints on how the material can be used in both formal and
informal liturgical settings are given in 'Some Hints on
Creating Liturgies' (see p. XVIII), together with ideas on how
to make imaginative use of available resources.

In order to honour copyright restrictions and to preserve the
integrity of the material, the language in this book is, on rare
occasions, exclusive. Generally, making language *inclusive*
(e.g. substituting 'people' or 'folk' for 'men', 'humankind' for
'mankind', 'children of God' for 'sons of God') is not difficult,
and it is hoped that people will feel free to adapt the wording
in this book, both for public and private use, where
appropriate.

If you know what you are looking for, there are three ways to
find it in this book:

1. You can look up the first line of an item in the Contents list at the beginning of the book. (It will save time if you know which of the eight themes the item is likely to come under.)
2. For material on a specific theme, you can turn to the Thematic Index at the back of the book. This lists the contents of each of the eight sections, together with alternative material relevant to each theme from elsewhere in the book. Symbols are also used throughout the book to indicate where an item has an alternative theme to that under which it is grouped.
3. For material of a specific type (e.g. prayers, songs, readings) you can use the Type Index, also at the back of the book. Here material is grouped first by its type and then by its theme.

Whether creating a liturgy or simply browsing, it is hoped that readers will find their way around this book with ease.

# KEY TO SYMBOLS

1. Environment and Land

2. Basic Needs

3. The Excluded

4. Conflict, War and Peace

5. Work and Debt

6. Women

7. Solidarity

8. Celebrating Hope

# Environment
## and Land

The earth is the Lord's and all that is in it,
the world and those who live in it;
For he has founded the seas,
and established it on the rivers.

*Psalm 24:1*

꘏

We often sing in church about the wonders and glory of
creation, about the things which God's hands have made. But
do our lives reflect the awe that we proclaim? Do we really
glory in creation and respect God's handiwork?

These poems and prayers challenge our thinking and the way
we live our lives. They question our confused understanding of
development. We seem intent on a headlong rush towards
industrialization that precludes developing a sustainable
lifestyle in harmony with our surroundings.

We are here for only a short time, but we leave heavy
footprints on the face of creation. We have lived for too long
simply taking from the environment, using and exploiting its
resources, not nurturing and cherishing the earth as God
intended us to.

Now is the time for a radical re-think. We can look to the
Bible for inspiration and to the indigenous peoples of the South
for guidance. Their understanding of the created order and
their deference towards it challenge our arrogant assumption
of ownership. The world and its resources – the water, the air,
the land and the trees – are not ours. They belong to God, who
asks us to be good stewards of his creation. Our prayer
challenges the greed that leads to destruction. It asks that we
should live more simply that others may simply live.

꘏

1. O Lord, O God,
   Creator of our land,
   our earth, the trees,
   the animals and humans,
   all is for your honour.
   The drums beat it out,
   and the people sing about it,
   and they dance with noisy joy
   that you are the Lord.

You also have pulled the other continents
out of the sea.
What a wonderful world you have made
out of wet mud,
and what beautiful men and women!

We thank you for all the beauty of this earth.
The grace of your creation is like a cool day
between rainy seasons.
We drink in your creation with our eyes,
we listen to the birds' jubilee
with our ears.
How strong and good
and sure your earth smells,
and everything that grows there.

Bless us.
Bless our land and people.
Bless our forests with mahogany,
wawa, and cacao.
Bless our fields with cassava and peanuts.
Bless the waters
that flow through our land.
Fill them with fish
and drive great schools of fish to our seacoast,
so that the fishermen in their unsteady boats
do not need to go out too far.

Be with us youth in our countries,
and in all Africa,
and in the whole world.
Prepare us for the service that we should render.

**Creator of our land**
*Ashanti people, Ghana*

2. In the beginning,
   in the very beginning,
   God gave birth to,
   God delivered,
   God created
   the heavens and the earth.
   Yes, out of the womb
   of fertile divinity
   emerged our mother,
   the earth.

Mother earth, sister sea, giving birth, energy,
reaching out, touching me lovingly.

**In the beginning**
*Miriam Therese Winter, USA*

3. God saw all he had made, and indeed, it was very good.
   Evening came and morning came: the sixth day.

   *Genesis 1:31*

**4.** Ripped from the land? What then?
Raised from the ground? How so?
As beneath your feet the ground
Like water slipping through your hand?

Like running the road in a dream?
Slipping in a single spot?
Like losing your footing in a dream
And falling to the hollow earth?

Ripped from the land? What then?
Raised from the ground? How so?
As under your feet the earth
Like water in the palm of your hand?

Living in bottomless mud?
Like lying in a bed of dust?
In a hammock swinging without a hammock
Seeing the world upside-down?

Floating farmer? Is that it?
Heavenly pastures? A celestial corral?
A flock in the clouds? But how?
Winged cattle? Ethereal stallions?

So odd a tillage! But how?
Ploughed fields in heaven? Can it be?
What orange, what apple will rain down?
Buds? Nectar? Hail? Manna?

**Raised from the ground**
*Chico Buarque (translated by Clifford Landers), Brazil*

5. If the land could speak,
   it would speak for us.
   It would say, like us, that the years
   have forged the bond of life that ties us together.
   It was our labour that made the land what she is;
   and it was her yielding that gave us life.
   We and the land are one.

   But who would listen?
   Will they listen,
   those invisible,
   who from an unfeeling distance, claim
   the land is theirs?
   Because pieces of paper say so?
   Because the pieces of paper are backed by men
   who speak threatening words;
   Men who have power to shoot and kill;
   men who have power to take our men and our sons away?

   If the land could speak,
   it would speak for us!
   For the land is us!
   And we speak!
   But who will listen?

   *Kalinga tribal people, Philippines*

6. Pilgrim God,
   You trod where others dared not tread,
   you spoke for those whose voices were not heard
   and walked the way of the cross to lay claim to Golgotha.
   So lead us through the wilderness of apathy
   that our whimpers of despair become cries of protest,
   our faltering footsteps become strides of purpose
   and our blind eyes become visions of hope,

that with the landless of the earth
we may enter Golgotha to songs of resurrection,
feel its death pains turn to birth pangs,
watch its dry land burst forth and bloom
and hear your pilgrim people rejoice and sing.

**A prayer for the earth's landless people**
Annabel Shilson-Thomas, United Kingdom

7. The Penang, a nomadic hunting and gathering people of
Sarawak, issued this appeal to the Sarawak Government:

*Stop destroying the forest or we will be forced to
protect it. The forest is our livelihood. We have lived
here before any of you outsiders came. We fished in
clean rivers and hunted in the jungle. We made our
sago meat and ate the fruit of the trees. Our life was
not easy, but we lived it content. Now the logging
companies turn rivers into muddy streams and the
jungle into devastation. The fish cannot survive in
dirty rivers and wild animals will not live in
devastated forest ... You take away our livelihood
and threaten our very lives. We want our ancestral land,
the land we live off, back. We can use it in a wiser way.
When you come, come to us as guests, with respect!*

The appeal went unheeded.

*The Penang people of Sarawak, Malaysia*

8. At the heart of everything is land. The land is my mother, the land gives protection, enjoyment and provides for our needs, economic, social and religious. We belong to the land in a true sense that it is a part of us. Just as you need your home and place and protect it, we need land and want to look after it.

*Aboriginal people, Australia*

9. Land will not be sold absolutely, for the land belongs to me, and you are only strangers and guests of mine.

*Leviticus 25:23*

10. Lord God, creator of all the earth, you have given us the mountains and trees, the waters and the good earth which supports our crops, our animals and ourselves. Never let us lose our love for our land, which is our mother. Help us to protect the land from abuse and to enrich the soil when we abuse it. Make our mother the earth fruitful again.

*Philippines*

11. So long
      as car-parks take
      precedence over hospitals,
      multi-storeyed hotels
      over homes for people,
      irrelevant factories
      over the paddy-fields
      of our daily sustenance,

I shall
sing no celebratory song ...

So long
as blind bulldozers
are allowed unchecked
to gouge our landscape,
and multinationals
are licensed to run
amok across this land,

I shall
sing no celebratory song ...

So long
as our rivers and streams,
our beaches, our air,
our oceans and trees,
our birds, our fish,
our butterflies and bees
are strangled, stifled,
polluted, poisoned,
crushed, condemned
by lop-sided development,

I shall
sing no celebratory song ...

No matter
how many suns go down,
this tongue
will be of thistle and thorn
until they right the wrong.

**No celebratory song**
*Cecil Rajendra, Malaysia*

**12.** And the smog and the radioactive material fell on the seas and the dry land and contaminated every herb yielding seed and every fruit tree yielding fruit.

And Man said, 'It is not very good, but we cannot put the clock back.'

This was the fifth day before the end.

And by his work, Man created great deserts and changed climatic conditions so that winds swept dust off the earth skywards to mingle with the smog, which blotted out the sun by day and the moon by night, so that night and day became the same.

And Man saw the work of his hands and said, 'Our conquest of Nature is almost complete.'

And this was the fourth day before the end.

The third day before the end Man said, 'Let us dump our industrial effluents, raw sewage and garbage into the streams and waterways and seas.'

And it was so.

The waters upon the earth became foul so that all life in the waters died.

*Professor E. Just, United Kingdom*

**13.** We in the Third World are destroying our environment. We cut down the wood to make fuel to cook. We cut the wood to sell to the cities to make a living. In 15 years there will be no trees left in Ghana...

I tell you: there is only one way to solve the threat to the environment. Poverty must be eliminated. How? You must have less. We must have more. You must sacrifice to give. You must give out of love.

*Bernard Guri, Ghana*

**14.** To plant a tree is to say Yes to life:
It is to affirm our faith in the future.

To plant a tree is to acknowledge our debt to the past:
Seeds are not created out of nothing.

To plant a tree is to co-operate in Nature's work
Whereby all forms of life are interdependent.

To plant a tree is a token of sorrow for past mistakes:
When we took life's gifts for granted.

To plant a tree is to make a social statement
For green-consciousness, for conservation and ecology.

To plant a tree is to enhance the quality of life:
It brings beauty to the eyes and uplift to the spirit.

To plant a tree is to make a spiritual point:
We are all members of the Tree of Life, we stand or
    fall together.

*Rev. Francis Simon, United Kingdom*

15. *Leader:* Every part of this shining earth is sacred.
    *All:* **Every shining pine needle, every sandy shore.**

    Every mist in the dark woods,
    **Every clearing and humming insect is holy.**

    Every rocky crest, the juices of the meadow, the beasts
        and all the people,
    **All belong to the same family.**

    Teach your children that the earth is our mother.
    **Whatever befalls the earth befalls the children of earth.**

    The water's murmur is the voice of our father's father.
    **We are part of the earth and the earth is part of us.**

    The rivers are our brothers; they quench our thirst.
    **The perfumed flowers are our sisters.**

    The air is precious,
    **For all of us share the same breath.**

    The wind that gave our grandparents breath also receives
        their last sigh.
    **The wind that gave our children the spirit of life.**

    This we know: the earth does not belong to us.
    **We belong to the earth.**

    This we know: all things are connected,
    **Like the blood which unites one family.**

    All things are connected.
    **Our God is the same God, whose compassion is equal
        for all.**

For we did not weave the web of life:
**We are merely a strand in it.**

Whatever we do to the web
**We do to ourselves.**

Let us give thanks for the web and the circle that
  connects us.
**Thanks be to God, the God of all.**

*A Litany of the Circle*
*Based on Chief Seattle's testimony, North America*

16. Recognizing that the earth and the fullness
    thereof is a gift from our gracious God, and that
    we are called to cherish, and nurture and provide
    loving stewardship for the earth's resources, and
    recognizing that life itself is a gift, and a call to
    responsibility, joy and celebration:

We declare ourselves to be world citizens.

We commit ourselves to lead ecologically sound lives.

We commit ourselves to lead lives of creative simplicity,
and to share our personal wealth with the world's poor.

We commit ourselves to join with others in reshaping
institutions so as to bring about a more just global society.

We will seek to avoid the creation of products which will
cause harm to others.

We affirm the gift of our body, and commit ourselves to its
proper nourishment and physical well-being.

We commit ourselves to examine continually our relations with others, and to attempt to relate honestly, morally and lovingly to those around us.

We commit ourselves to personal renewal through prayer, meditation and study.

We promise responsible participation in a community of faith.

*Shakertown pledge, USA*

# 17. ALL PRAISE TO YOU

1. All praise to you, O Lord of all cre - a - tion;
You made the world, and it is yours a - lone.
The pla - net earth you spun on its lo - ca - tion
a - mid the stars a - dorn - ing hea - ven's dome.

Words: Omer Westendorf (b. 1916). © 1984 World Library Publications, Inc., a division of J. S. Paluch Company, Inc., 3825 N. Willow Rd, Schiller Park, IL 60176, USA. All rights reserved
Music: *Finlandia*, Jean Sibelius (1865–1957). Breitkopf und Härtel, Wiesbaden, Leipzig, Germany. Used by permission

We lease the earth but for a life's du-ra-tion,_____

Yet for this life it is our trea-sured home._____

1. All praise to you, O Lord of all creation;
   You made the world, and it is yours alone.
   The planet earth you spun on its location
   amid the stars adorning heaven's dome.
   We lease the earth but for a life's duration,
   Yet for this life it is our treasured home.

2. With wondrous grace you clothed the earth in splendour;
   with teeming life you filled the sea and land.
   Instil in us a sense of awe and wonder,
   when we behold the bounty of your hand.
   Then when we hear the voice of bird or thunder,
   we hear the voice our faith can understand.

3. To tend the earth is our entrusted duty,
   for earth is ours to use and not abuse.
   O gracious Lord, true source of all resources,
   forgive our greed, that wields destruction's sword.
   Then let us serve as wise and faithful stewards
   while earth gives glory to creation's Lord.

# 18. MANY AND GREAT

**Mysteriously**

1. Ma - ny and great, O God, are your works,

Ma - ker of earth and sky;

your hands have set the hea - vens with stars;

your fin - gers spread the moun - tains and plains.

You mere - ly spoke and wa - ters were formed;

deep seas o - bey your voice.

Words: Dakota Indian hymn, paraphrased by Philip Frazier (1892–1964), © Walton Music Corp.
Music: Traditional Native American melody

1. Many and great, O God, are your works,
   Maker of earth and sky;
   your hands have set the heavens with stars;
   your fingers spread the mountains and plains.
   You merely spoke and waters were formed;
   deep seas obey your voice.

2. Grant now to us communion with you,
   O star-abiding one;
   come now to us and stay by our side.
   With you are found the true gifts of life.
   Bless us with life that has no end,
   eternal life with you.

See also material from Section 8, *Celebrating Hope*

# 19. GOD, BEYOND ALL NAMES

♩ = 54–58
INTRO
Capo 3(Em)

VERSES 1–3, 5

1. God, be-yond our dreams, you have stirred in us a me-mory, you have placed your power-ful spi-rit in the hearts of hu - man - kind.

REFRAIN

All a -

*The guitar accompaniment is not compatible with the organ accompaniment.

Words and music: © 1990 Bernadette Farrell, published by OCP Publications,
5536 NE Hassolo, Portland, Oregon 97213, USA. All rights reserved. Used by permission

VERSE 4

4. God, be-yond all time, you are la-bour-ing with-in us; we are
mov-ing, we are chang-ing in your spi-rit, ev-er new. All a-
-round us we have known you, all cre - a-tion lives to hold you. In our
liv-ing and our dy-ing we are bring-ing you to birth.

D.S.

1. God, beyond our dreams,
   you have stirred in us a memory,
   you have placed your powerful spirit
   in the hearts of humankind.

*Refrain:*
   All around us we have known you,
   all creation lives to hold you.
   In our living and our dying
   we are bringing you to birth.

2. God, beyond all names,
   you have made us in your image;
   we are like you, we reflect you;
   we are woman, we are man.

*Refrain*

3. God, beyond all words,
   all creation tells your story;
   you have shaken with our laughter,
   you have trembled with our tears.

*Refrain*

4. God, beyond all time,
   you are labouring within us;
   we are moving, we are changing
   in your spirit, ever new.

*Refrain*

5. God of tender care,
   you have cradled us in goodness,
   you have mothered us in wholeness,
   you have loved us into birth.

*Refrain*


See also material from Section 6, *Women*

# 20. THINK OF A WORLD

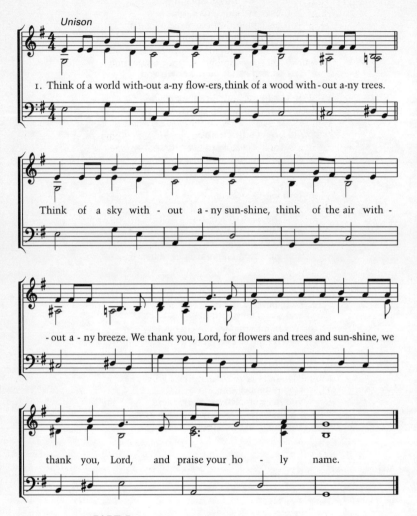

1. Think of a world with-out a-ny flow-ers, think of a wood with-out a-ny trees.

Think of a sky with-out a-ny sun-shine, think of the air with-

-out a-ny breeze. We thank you, Lord, for flowers and trees and sun-shine, we

thank you, Lord, and praise your ho - ly name.

**PART I**

1. Think of a world without any flowers,
    think of a wood without any trees.
    Think of a sky without any sunshine,
    think of the air without any breeze.
    We thank you, Lord, for flowers and trees and sunshine,
    we thank you, Lord, and praise your holy name.

Words: Doreen Newport © 1969 Stainer & Bell Ltd. Used by permission
Music: Graham Westcott © 1973 Stainer & Bell Ltd. Used by permission

2. Think of a world without any animals,
   think of a field without any herd.
   Think of a stream without any fishes,
   think of a dawn without any bird.
   We thank you, Lord, for all your living creatures,
   we thank you, Lord, and praise your holy name.

3. Think of a world without any paintings,
   think of a room where all the walls are bare.
   Think of a rainbow without any colours,
   think of the earth with darkness everywhere.
   We thank you, Lord, for paintings and for colours,
   we thank you, Lord, and praise your holy name.

## PART 2

4. Think of a world without any poetry,
   think of a book without any words.
   Think of a song without any music,
   think of a hymn without any verse.
   We thank you, Lord, for poetry and music,
   we thank you, Lord, and praise your holy name.

5. Think of a world without any science,
   think of a journey with nothing to explore.
   Think of a quest without any mystery,
   nothing to seek and nothing left in store.
   We thank you, Lord, for miracles of science,
   we thank you, Lord, and praise your holy name.

6. Think of a world without any people,
   think of a street with no one living there.
   Think of a town without any houses,
   no one to love and nobody to care.
   We thank you, Lord, for families and friendships,
   we thank you, Lord, and praise your holy name.

## PART 3

7. Think of a world without any worship,
   think of a God without his only Son.
   Think of a cross without a resurrection,
   only a grave and not a victory won.
   We thank you, Lord, for showing us our Saviour,
   we thank you, Lord, and praise your holy name.

8. Thanks to our Lord for being here among us,
   thanks be to you for sharing all we do.
   Thanks for our church and all the love we find here,
   thanks for this place and all its promise true.
   We thank you, Lord, for life in all its richness,
   we thank you, Lord, and praise your holy name.

See also material from Section 8, *Celebrating Hope*

# Basic
# Needs

Give us this day our daily bread.

*Matthew 6:11*

 

—

 

We have all seen the statistics. They tell us that the gap between rich and poor is getting wider and wider. But statistics are faceless. They deal in numbers, not people, and are easy to ignore. But people, unlike figures on paper, cannot be filed away. Their presence is real.

Christ's presence is real. We encounter him in each faceless number we meet: the hungry, the sick, the stranger and the prisoner (Matthew 25:37–40). In this section we share their stories, and discover the reality of poverty in a world where a rich minority have everything that money can buy.

We pray for a change of priorities, for a global society where the needs of the poor and powerless come before the demands of the rich and powerful. We pray that when we make our everyday choices – for example, how we shop, how we vote and what we say – we will think of their effect on the poor and make our choices count.

Poverty and hunger are not inevitable; they are the outcome of society's choice to favour the rich over the poor. As the prophets of old challenged the rich to think of the needs of the poor, we too are challenged by the poor to change. We can make a difference through our prayers, our attitudes and our actions.

—

1. It is not enough to conquer hunger
   or put an end to poverty.
   Our goal must be to build a world –
   a world developed to the full,
   so much so, that all men and women,
   no matter what their race or creed,
   can live a truly human life.
   Our goal must be, for every man and woman,
   a life set free from all oppression.
   Our goal must be, for every man and woman,
   a life strong enough
   to master nature, and be free.
   Our goal must be
   a world where liberty is real;
   a world where Lazarus
   can sit at Dives' table.

   *Pope Paul VI*

2. I was homeless, but you said to me,
   'Birds of the air have nests,
   But the Son of Man has nowhere to lay his head'
      (Matthew 8:22).

   I lack clothes to cover me, and you quickly retorted,
   'And why do you worry about clothes?
   See how the lilies of the field grow;
   They do not labour or spin' (Matthew 6:8).

   I was hungry; all you quoted to me was,
   'Jesus said: "I am the bread of life,
   He who comes to me will never go hungry!"' (John 6:35).

   I got sick because of malnutrition.
   'Trust in the Lord with all your heart!' (Proverbs 3:5).

'He forgives all my sins
and heals all my diseases' (Psalm 103:3).

Helpless, I stole food and medicine.
'He is our help', according to Psalm 33:20.
'Do not steal!' Matthew 19:18 explicitly commands.
'Because the Lord your God loves you'
   (Deuteronomy 23:5).

In prison, I wept and grieved.
Immediately you recited:
'You will grieve, but your grief will turn to joy'
   (John 16:20).

You are impressively biblical.
Praise God for you!
But I wish I could understand you,
Because I am still in prison –
Poor, homeless, naked, sick and grieved!

***To my spiritual brethren***
*Anton Iniguez, Malaya*

3. Forgive us, Lord our God, as we bicker over issues of
   canon law and liturgy while your children suffer and die.
   Amen.

*Sheila Cassidy, United Kingdom*

**4.** *Leader:* With the people of —, we remember the poor; those who struggle to feed hungry mouths and clothe malnourished bodies, who strive to make homes from discarded waste and build a future from shattered dreams. Lord, free us from our comfort, that with them we may work towards the coming of God's kingdom.

Blessed are the poor.
*All:* **The kingdom of heaven is theirs.**

With the people of —, we remember those who mourn; those whose hearts ache and whose memories torment, who grieve for parent, sister, partner, child, and who cry for themselves, for the lives they once knew and have now lost. Lord, free our tears that we may weep with them.

Blessed are those who mourn.
**They shall be comforted.**

With the people of —, we remember the meek; those who listen with intent and not with mild indifference, who persevere quietly where others make a noise, who brave the intolerable and seek to understand the different. Lord, free us from our fears, that we may let go of our prejudices.

Blessed are the meek.
**They shall inherit the earth.**

With the people of —, we remember those who hunger and thirst for righteousness; those who long for justice and fight in the face of despair, who are fired by anger and compassion to pursue a vision and create a future. Lord, free us from our passivity, that we may join their struggle.

Blessed are those who hunger and thirst for righteousness.
**They shall be satisfied.**

With the people of —, we remember the merciful; those who are wronged but seek not revenge, who are hurt and seek to understand the pain, who refuse to be crippled by self-pity, but grapple with confusion so that bridges can be built. Lord, free us from a desire to forget, that we may learn to forgive.

Blessed are the merciful.
**They shall have mercy shown to them.**

With the people of —, we remember the pure in heart; those who seek to listen rather than condemn, who refuse to blindly obey codes or live by rules, but who struggle to understand what is difficult and have the strength and courage to change. Lord, free us from self-righteousness, that we may embrace the fullness of life.

Blessed are the pure in heart.
**They shall see God.**

With the people of —, we remember the peacemakers; those who work for peace in the face of war, who strive for solutions in the wake of conflict, who refuse to be daunted by abuse of power, and build bridges in places where others dare not tread. Lord, free us from apathy, that we may actively pursue all that leads to peace.

Blessed are the peacemakers.
**They shall be called children of God.**

With the people of —, we remember those who are persecuted; those who have the courage to challenge and to speak the truth, who are driven by a desire for justice and are moved by a spirit of compassion. Lord, free us from our sterility, that we may be emboldened to love.

Blessed are the persecuted for righteousness' sake.
**The kingdom of heaven is theirs.**

*We remember*
*Annabel Shilson-Thomas, United Kingdom*

5. O mighty and merciful God,
   my family prays to You,
   glorifies and praises You,
   adores You and pleads with You.
   Here stands this small circle
   before Your great majesty.
   We would not dare to pray to You
   if Jesus had not said it was all right.

   Lord of Lords,
   we put ourselves
   under Your commands.
   Most of our family is still in the village.
   We are alone here in the city
   and do not feel at home yet.
   Many temptations and constant danger
   surround us.
   Lord,
   please watch over these little children
   when they go to school.
   Those trucks and taxis go much too fast.

   Lord, in this big city
   without friends
   we have only You to trust in.
   We are afraid to be without a job
   and of death.
   Lord,
   protect us in this city.
   We are at home wherever You are.
   Stay with us, we pray.
   Amen.

   *Source unknown, Ghana*

**6.** Then the righteous will answer him, 'Lord, when was it that we saw you hungry and gave you food, or thirsty and gave you something to drink? And when was it that we saw you a stranger and welcomed you, or naked and gave you clothing? And when was it that we saw you sick or in prison and visited you? And the king will answer them, "Truly I tell you, just as you did it to one of the least of these who are members of my family, you did it to me."'

*Matthew 25:37–40*

**7.** Apollo 2 cost more than Apollo 1,
Apollo 1 cost plenty.
Apollo 3 cost more than Apollo 2,
Apollo 2 cost more than Apollo 1,
Apollo 1 cost plenty.
Apollo 4 cost more than Apollo 3,
Apollo 3 cost more than Apollo 2,
Apollo 2 cost more than Apollo 1,
Apollo 1 cost plenty.

Apollo 8 cost a fortune, but no one minded
because the astronauts were Protestants
and from the moon they read the Bible
to the delight and edification of all Christians,
and on their return Pope Paul gave them his blessing.
Apollo 9 cost more than all of them put together,
and that includes Apollo 1, which cost plenty.
The great-grandparents of the people of Acahualinca
were less hungry than their grandparents.
The great-grandparents died of hunger.
The grandparents of the people of Acahualinca
were less hungry than their parents.
The grandparents died of hunger.

The parents of the people of Acahualinca
were less hungry than the people are today.
The parents died of hunger.
The people who live today in Acahualinca
are less hungry than their children.
The children of the people of Acahualinca
are not born because of hunger
and they hunger to be born
so they can die of hunger.
And that is what the people of Acahualinca do.
They die of hunger.
Blessed are the poor,
for they shall inherit the moon.

**The earth is a satellite of the moon**
*Leonel Rugama, Nicaragua*

8. When a man's stomach is full, it makes no difference if he
   is rich or poor.

   *Euripides*

9. Is not this the fast that I choose:
   to loose the bonds of injustice,
   to undo the thongs of the yoke,
   to let the oppressed go free,
   and to break the yoke?
   Is it not to share your bread with the hungry,
   and bring the homeless to your house;
   when you see the naked to cover them
   and not to hide yourself from your own kin?

   *Isaiah 58:6–7*

10. My name is Gary. But no one wants to know. I am
    homeless and everybody's stereotype. Sat in my doorway,
    I am all things to passers-by. To one I'm a drop-out,
    avoiding life's responsibilities. To another, an alcoholic or
    a junkie, frightening and disease ridden. To another I'm
    mentally ill. Or
    an aggressive beggar. A criminal, perhaps. To none am I an
    individual, and that's what really hurts. Homelessness is
    blamed on many things. But your callousness is your
    responsibility. I'm not just a 'homeless person', I am an
    individual. I'd like to talk to you, or anyone, about that,
    but no
    one is brave enough to tell me their name. My name is
    Gary, but no one …

    *Gary Gallard, United Kingdom*

11. Holy God, as you plucked up the people of Israel
    and set them down to build and to plant,
    so stretch out your life-giving hand to the dispossessed,
    that with our help they may build and plant,
    reap and sow, dance and sing.
    Fill them with courage to love,
    strength to rebuild and grace to grow,
    that once more they may rise up and cry freedom,
    may shake off the chains of oppression to wear dignity,
    and may leave behind the shackles of despair to
       embrace hope.

    **To build and to plant**
    *Annabel Shilson-Thomas, United Kingdom*

**12.** O God to those who have hunger give bread,
and to those who have bread give the hunger for justice.
Amen.

*Source unknown, Latin America*

**13.** When we rise each morning, we go to the bathroom
where we reach for a sponge which is provided by a
Pacific islander. We reach for soap that is created for
us by a European. Then at table we drink coffee which is
provided for us by a South American, or tea by a Chinese,
or cocoa by a West African. Before we leave for our jobs we
are already beholden to more than half the world.

*Martin Luther King Jr, USA.*

**14.** Lord of Creation,
moulder of our fragile clay,
shape us in your image.
Spin us round, if you must
until we're dizzy;
Hollow us out, if you must
until we're empty
of all that is false and useless.
Fill us daily with living water
that we may carry your life
to a world dying of thirst.

*Sheila Cassidy, United Kingdom*

15. All the broken hearts
    shall rejoice:
    all those
    who are heavy laden,
    whose eyes are tired
    and do not see,
    shall be lifted up
    to meet with
    the motherly healer.
    The battered souls and bodies
    shall be healed:
    the hungry
    shall be fed;
    the imprisoned
    shall be free;
    all earthly children
    shall regain joy
    in the reign
    of the just and loving one
    coming for you
    coming for me
    in this time
    in this world.

*Sun Ai Lee Park, Asia*

# 16. CHRIST, BE OUR LIGHT

Words and music: © 1993 Bernadette Farrell, published by OCP Publications,
5536 NE Hassolo, Portland, Oregon 97213, USA. All rights reserved. Used by permission

1. Longing for light, we wait in darkness.
   Longing for truth, we turn to you.
   Make us your own, your holy people,
   light for the world to see.

*Refrain:*
   Christ, be our light!
   Shine in our hearts.
   Shine through the darkness.
   Christ, be our light!
   Shine in your Church gathered today.

2. Longing for peace, our world is troubled.
   Longing for hope, many despair.
   Your word alone has power to save us.
   Make us your living voice.

*Refrain*

3. Longing for food, many are hungry.
   Longing for water, many still thirst.
   Make us your bread, broken for others,
   shared until all are fed.

*Refrain*

4. Longing for shelter, many are homeless.
   Longing for warmth, many are cold.
   Make us your building, sheltering others,
   walls made of living stone.

*Refrain*

5. Many the gifts, many the people,
   many the hearts that yearn to belong.
   Let us be servants to one another,
   making your kingdom come.

*Refrain*

See also material from Section 3, *The Excluded* and Section 7, *Solidarity*

# 17. WHEN I NEEDED A NEIGHBOUR

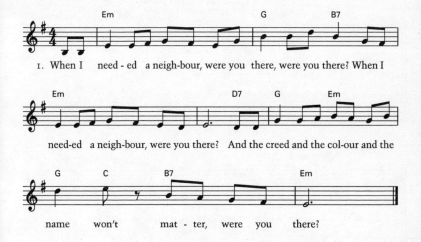

1. When I need-ed a neigh-bour, were you there, were you there? When I

need-ed a neigh-bour, were you there? And the creed and the col-our and the

name won't mat - ter, were you there?

1. When I needed a neighbour,
   were you there, were you there?
   When I needed a neighbour,
   were you there?
   And the creed and the colour
   and the name won't matter,
   were you there?

2. I was hungry and thirsty . . .

3. I was cold, I was naked . . .

4. When I needed a shelter . . .

5. When I needed a healer . . .

6. Wherever you travel,
   I'll be there, I'll be there.
   Wherever you travel,
   I'll be there.
   And the creed and the colour
   and the name won't matter,
   I'll be there.

See also material from Section 3, *The Excluded* and Section 7, *Solidarity*

Words and music: Sydney Carter. © 1965 Stainer & Bell Ltd. Used by permission

# 18. HERE IN THE BUSY CITY

1. Here in the bu-sy ci-ty now let the Church be seen where less-er gods are wor-shipped in mon-ey and ma-chine; where news is but sen-sa-tion, the Good News hard-ly heard; now let the Church take ac-tion in liv-ing out the Word!

Words: © 1983 Shirley Erena Murray. Used by permission
Music: *Merle's Tune*, Hal H. Hopson © 1983 Hope Publishing Company, administered by CopyCare Ltd,
PO Box 77, Hailsham, East Sussex BN27 3EF, UK. Used by permission

1. Here in the busy city now let the Church be seen
   where lesser gods are worshipped in money and machine;
   where news is but sensation, the Good News hardly heard;
   now let the Church take action in living out the Word!

2. In policies and planning, the Church be there to speak,
   to moderate the powerful, to argue for the weak:
   where law must sit in judgement and love is little known,
   there at the crisis centre the Christ's concern be shown.

3. Where litter chokes the gutter and people go to waste,
   where joblessness is bitter and living lost its taste,
   to under-leavened people be proof of rising yeast,
   in lives devoid of flavour be saltiness released!

4. Here in the busy city God walks on every street
   in generous or greedy, the honest or the cheat,
   and daily we must offer the good that goes unpriced,
   with vigour and with vision the lifestyle of the Christ.

See also material from Section 5, *Work and Debt*

# The
# Excluded

The Lord is near to the broken-hearted
and saves the crushed in spirit.

*Psalm 34:18*

The excluded. Who are they? They are the people we don't like
to think about too much. We walk past them in the street as
they huddle in doorways. They are the people who have
nothing, at a time when conspicuous consumption is
everything.

The world is divided into people who have everything they
need and a majority left with little or nothing. They're
excluded; on the outside, looking in. If we're on the inside we
build barriers, like invisible but impenetrable walls. Inside the
walls are the people who are the 'right' colour, who speak the
'right' language, follow the 'right' religious practices, and have
enough money to be consumers. They may, at certain times of
the year, feel sorry for those on the outside and, through a
chink in the wall, pass out some clothes they don't need any
more, or some sandwiches which have only just passed their
sell-by date. They are too afraid to go out.

But we should never forget that Jesus was born in the poorest
surroundings, to an unmarried mother, and spent his life as an
itinerant preacher. Have we built up so many barriers in our
world that we are too afraid to go outside to meet him? We
pray for open hearts and open minds, we pray that we may
learn to make room for everyone and turn no one away.

1. Oh God, oh why aren't we heard with our voices?
   We cry aloud but we are not heard.
   Oh why, oh why do we do as we are told by people
   of authority, but we are not heard?
   Oh why, oh why do they take our children away from us?
   Oh why, oh why do they put our children in children's
     homes?
   Oh why, oh why do they take our parenting rights away
     from us?
   Oh why, oh why do we suffer in silence?
   Oh why, oh why do we feel ashamed?
   Oh why, oh why do we feel as if we had committed a
     crime?
   Oh why, oh why do we hide ourselves from humanity?
   Oh why, oh why aren't we heard with our voices?
   We cry aloud but we are not heard.
   Oh why, oh why can't we unite
   and LET US BE HEARD!

   *Seamus Neville, United Kingdom*

2. We can turn away and avoid seeing. We can
   rejoice that we still have the protection of our
   skin and bones. We can make our body into a
   shield, a walking barricade, and hide behind it. How
   unendurable, if we only had our soul! A soul can't turn
   away, it can't cover itself up. It can't even shut its eyes.
   It's always on view. Whereas we are all right, we are well
   provided for. We can stuff our ears, we can withdraw into
   ourselves; and if things are really bad – turn to the wall
   and use our good solid backs to cover from behind.

   **Unguarded thoughts**
   *Andrew Sinyavskycou, Russia*

3. Creator God, open our eyes to the hopes and needs
   of all the people we meet. Help us to learn about
   Africa without judgement or despair. Give us the
   courage to respond with justice and respect, and
   together let's build your Kingdom of Love.

   We pray for those who are suffering this day from hunger,
   poor housing, unemployment, loneliness and despair as a
   result of neglect and injustice; may their spirits not be
   broken by their bodies' pain.

   Jesus Christ, friend of the poor and lonely, we give you
   thanks for the opportunity to share the lives of the people
   of Africa, whose lives are burdened by circumstances
   beyond their control. We pray that our work may help to
   bring comfort and hope to these people in need as we seek
   your Kingdom of Peace on earth.

   *Jimmy Palso (adapted), South Africa*

4. *Leader:* Lord, you entered Jerusalem to cheers of
   'Hosanna!' and left with your cross to cries of 'Crucify!'

   We remember the times when we have made you in our
   own image, the times when we have called our own
   aspirations yours, the times when we have misunderstood
   the way of the cross and have deceived ourselves and
   others.

   Give us strength to journey with you and grace to discern
   the way that is yours.
   Lord of the cross,
   *All:* **forgive us and heal us.**

Lord, you overturned the tables of the temple money-changers. You said, 'My house shall be called a house of prayer.'

We remember the times when we have failed to make connections between our lives and our faith, the times when we have remained complacent and inert in the face of injustice and have violated your bodily temple by our selfishness and greed.

Inspire us to work for justice and fill us with the desire to build an integrated community of faith.
Lord of the cross,
**forgive us and heal us.**

Lord, you were anointed by an unknown woman in preparation for burial.

We remember the times when we have been too busy to love you, the times when we have failed to recognize your needs in others, the times when we have made ordinary that which is special and dismissed that which is precious.

Impassion us with the love of the unknown woman, that we may serve you in friend and stranger.
Lord of the cross,
**forgive us and heal us.**

Lord, you humbly took a towel and washed the feet of your friends.

We remember the times when we have fought for prominence, the times when we have desired power and have forgotten those without a voice, the times when we have pursued our own freedom and have enslaved others.

Give us courage to embrace your service freely, to take up
your cross and follow you.
Lord of the cross,
**forgive us and heal us.**

Lord, you knew that Peter, who called you the Christ,
would deny you three times.

We remember the times when we have denied you and
have been afraid to speak the truth, the times when we
have followed the path of safety and have ignored the path
of risk.

Empower us to change, to become the rock on which you
build your Church, that we may go forth to proclaim your
kingdom and build up the body of Christ.
Lord of the cross,
**forgive us and heal us
and make us one in heart and mind
to serve you in humility. Amen.**

*Intercessions for holy week*
*Annabel Shilson-Thomas, United Kingdom*

5. went to an all black school
   with an all black name
   all black principal
   black teacher
   graduated
   with an all black concept

   with our blackety blackety frustration
   we did an all black march
   with high black hopes
   with an all black song

got a few solutions
not all black

went to a show
and saw our struggles
in black and white

Lawwwwwd have mercy

***Black and white***
*Michael Smith, Caribbean*

6. Leader: Before the fear of HIV/AIDS
we ask for the courage to love,
that compassion may triumph over hysteria,
reason over hatred,
joy over despair.
All: **We ask for courage**.

In the presence of HIV/AIDS
we ask for perseverance in love,
that the bonds of kinship and friendship,
the bonds of humanity may be proven strong and true.
**We ask for perseverance**.

In the reality of HIV/AIDS
we ask for healing,
the healing of the body and the spirit,
the healing of a blighted future.
**We ask for healing**.

In the extremity of HIV/AIDS,
we give thanks for those whose lives speak love,
whose acts dispel prejudice,
whose joy overcomes fear.
**We give thanks**.

As HIV/AIDS recognizes no distinctions
of gender or age,
nationality or sexual orientation,
race or creed, guilt or innocence,
neither do we.
We ask for the will to face up to HIV/AIDS,
the knowledge to conquer it,
and the grace to enhance our humanity.
**Amen**.

*Prayer for World Aids Day*
*CAFOD, United Kingdom*

7. You may be in another country,
   a country which is very rich,
   but if you have no homeland to go back to,
   you are still in the bush.

   Away from your homeland,
   any person can treat you as if you were worthless.
   Away from your homeland,
   you endure the life of a homeless person.
   Away from your homeland,
   you are subject to prejudice and misunderstanding.

   Away from your homeland, your trust is spoiled.
   Away from your homeland,
   you become useless in the eyes of others.
   Away from your homeland,
   you are forced to persevere and pass through disaster.
   Away from your homeland,
   you are like a baby that has been weaned.

   Away from your homeland,
   you may be disowned by your friends.

Away from your homeland,
you are devoured like a docile animal that has no teeth.
Away from your homeland,
you become like a docile animal that has been tamed.
Away from your homeland,
your soul knows deep sorrow.
Away from your homeland,
life appears useless, useless, too useless.

**Home is home and bush is bush**
*Bartholomew Bo Deng, Kakuma camp, Sudan*

8. Used, abused and throwaway,
   you are the children of the streets.

   Hearts of stone have never known
   the love you never had.

   Rough and tough, street-wise,
   to survive you flash and snatch
   just enough to stay alive.
   At eight years old, you are never told
   the right you have to be.

   Throwaway children of the streets,
   I hear your silent tears,
   I see you sleep exhausted,
   I know your deepest fears.

   Bundled rags are stirring from
   drug-induced forgetfulness
   near the railway arch.

   Runaway, Runaway,
   frightened to go home.

Throwaway children,
the lonely streets to roam.

Fretted sleep in parents' 'loving
arms' turns to wakeful fright
when tender touch pulls down
the veil of innocence
and childhood ends.

Then hidden anger and imagined guilts
shape your troubled smile.
The fear of adults lingers on,
without comfort or compassion,
as a heedless world
turns the page – and yawns.

**Throwaway children**
*Shay Cullen, Philippines*

9. I pray for the ones who help me. I pray that the
   word of God will spread and live long. I pray for
   rain and food, because there are so many people who have
   neither. I pray for more justice and peace in this world.

**Mana's Prayer**
*Mana is a 58-year-old Ethiopian who has Hansen's disease
(leprosy), Ethiopia*

10. The *guerrillero* came down from the mountain
               his tongue was the book of Exodus
           eyes opened like the gospels
                  and he was in need of a shave.

clothed in a red T-shirt, denim jeans, base-
ball cap and bearing the stigmata
                         on his hands, feet and side
needing help as only a saviour can;
                              he placed concepts
like plastic explosives
                    against military installations
that we had set up around our hearts


                    fears fled before him like
          vanquished *guardia nacional*


one *campesino*, a man called Tomás,
                         didn't ... couldn't
believe at first
                    but once he had touched the
beautiful wounds
          he knew and was radicalized by love.

*Bill Lewis, United Kingdom*

———

**11.** In Christ there is neither Jew nor Greek, there is
neither slave nor free, there is neither male nor
female: for you are all one in Christ Jesus.

*Galatians 3:28*

———

**12.** You ask me, what did I dream?
I dreamt I became
a bird.
You ask me, why did I
want to become a bird?
I really wanted to
have wings.

You ask me, why did I
want wings?
These wings would
help me fly back to
my country.
You ask me, why did I
want to go back there?
Because I wanted to
find something
I missed.

You ask me, what
do I miss?
I miss the place where
I lived as a child.
You ask me, what was
that place like?
The place was happy,
my family was close
together.

You ask me, what do I
remember best?
I still remember my
father reading the
newspaper.
You ask me, why do I
think of him?

I miss him and
I'm sad.

You ask me, why
I am sad?
I'm sad because all my
friends have fathers.
You ask me, why does
this matter?
Because my father is
far away.
I want to fly to him
like a bird.

**Dream of a bird**
*14-year-old Vietnamese boy, Australia*

---

13. *Leader:* Lord, we confess our day-to-day failure
to be human.
*All:* **Lord, we confess to you.**

Lord, we confess that we often fail to love with all that we
have and are, often because we do not fully understand what
loving means, often because we are afraid of risking ourselves.
**Lord, we confess to you.**

Lord, we cut ourselves off from each other and we erect
barriers of division.
**Lord, we confess to you.**

Lord, we confess that by silence and ill-considered words
**we have built up walls of prejudice.**

Lord, we confess that by selfishness and lack of sympathy
**we have stifled generosity and left little time for others.**

Holy Spirit, speak to us. Help us listen to your word of forgiveness, for we are very deaf.
**Come fill this moment and free us from our sin.**

*A litany of confession*
*Cathedral Church of Saint George, Cape Town, South Africa*

# 14. JESUS CHRIST IS WAITING

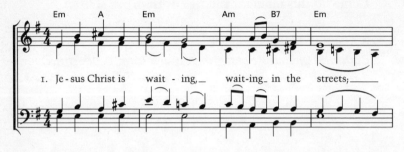

1. Je-sus Christ is wait - ing,— wait-ing— in the streets;—

no one is his neigh - bour, all— a - lone he eats.—

Lis - ten, Lord Je - sus, I am lone - ly too.—

Make me, friend or stran - ger,— fit— to— wait on you.

*The guitar accompaniment is not compatible with the vocal harmonies.

Words: The Iona Community. © WGRG Iona Community, Glasgow
Music: *Noël Nouvelet* (French traditional melody) arranged by
The Iona Community. © WGRG Iona Community, Glasgow

1. Jesus Christ is waiting,
   waiting in the streets;
   no one is his neighbour,
   all alone he eats.
   Listen, Lord Jesus,
   I am lonely too.
   Make me, friend or stranger,
   fit to wait on you.

2. Jesus Christ is raging,
   raging in the streets,
   where injustice spirals
   and real hope retreats.
   Listen, Lord Jesus,
   I am angry too.
   In the kingdom's causes,
   let me rage with you.

3. Jesus Christ is healing,
   healing in the streets,
   curing those who suffer,
   touching those he greets.
   Listen, Lord Jesus,
   I have pity too.
   Let my care be active,
   healing just like you.

4. Jesus Christ is dancing,
   dancing in the streets,
   where each sign of hatred
   he, with love, defeats.
   Listen, Lord Jesus,
   I should triumph too.
   On suspicion's graveyard,
   let me dance with you.

5. Jesus Christ is calling,
   calling in the streets,
   'Who will join my journey?
   I will guide their feet.'
   Listen, Lord Jesus,
   let my fears be few.
   Walk one step before me,
   I will follow you.

See also material from Section 7, *Solidarity*

# 15. A TOUCHING PLACE

1. Christ's is the world in which we move, Christ's are the folk we're sum-moned to love, Christ's is the voice which calls us to care,_ and Christ is the one who meets us here. To the lost Christ shows his face; to the un - loved he gives his em - brace;_ to those who cry__ in pain or dis - grace,_ Christ

Words: John L. Bell and Graham Maule. © WGRG Iona Community, Glasgow
Music: *Dream Angus* (Scottish traditional melody), arranged by
The Iona Community. © WGRG Iona Community, Glasgow

makes, with his friends, a touch - ing place._

1. Christ's is the world in which we move,
   Christ's are the folk we're summoned to love,
   Christ's is the voice which calls us to care,
   and Christ is the one who meets us here.

*Refrain:*
   To the lost Christ shows his face;
   to the unloved he gives his embrace;
   to those who cry in pain or disgrace,
   Christ makes, with his friends, a touching place.

2. Feel for the people we most avoid,
   strange or bereaved or never employed;
   feel for the women, and feel for the men
   who fear that their living is all in vain.

*Refrain*

3. Feel for the parents who've lost their child,
   feel for the women whom men have defiled,
   feel for the baby for whom there's no breast,
   and feel for the weary who find no rest.

*Refrain*

4. Feel for the lives by life confused,
   riddled with doubt, in loving abused;
   feel for the lonely heart, conscious of sin,
   which longs to be pure but fears to begin.

*Refrain*

See also material from Section 7, *Solidarity*

# 16. GOD BLESS THE GRASS

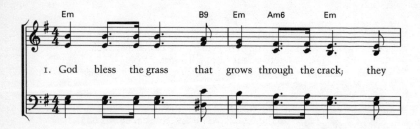

1. God bless the grass that grows through the crack; they

roll the con-crete ov - er it to try to keep it back. The

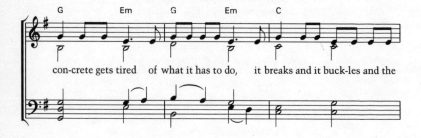

con-crete gets tired of what it has to do, it breaks and it buck-les and the

grass grows through, and God bless the grass.

Words and music: Malvina Reynolds © 1968 Schroder Music Company. Used by permission

1. God bless the grass that grows through the crack;
   they roll the concrete over it to try to keep it back.
   The concrete gets tired of what it has to do,
   it breaks and it buckles and the grass grows through,
   and God bless the grass.

2. God bless the truth that fights towards the sun.
   They heap the lies all over it and think that it is done.
   It moves through the ground and reaches for the air,
   and after a while it is growing everywhere,
   and God bless the grass.

3. God bless the grass that grows through cement.
   It's green and very tender and it's easily bent.
   But after a while it raises up its head
   for grass is a living thing and stone is dead,
   and God bless the grass.

4. God bless the grass that's gentle and low.
   Its roots are very deep and its plan wills it to grow.
   God bless the truth, the friend of the poor,
   and the wild grass that grows at the forgotten door,
   and God bless the grass.

See also material from Section 1, *Environment and Land* and Section 6, *Women*

# Conflict, War and Peace

Blessed are the peace makers, for they will be called the children of God.

*Matthew 5:9*

—

Emmanuel is ten. He was born in a refugee camp to the sound of gunfire. His father has been killed by a landmine. His mother prostitutes herself in a desperate attempt to feed Emmanuel and his younger sister. His elder brother, just twelve years old, has joined the rebel army. Their world is one of struggle and conflict.

Thousands of miles away a pre-Raphaelite Jesus stares benignly from a stained-glass window, his gentle, mild features conveying the view that peace is passive and individual, clean and sanitized, not active and communal, messy and hard won.

Just as colonialism bequeathed this distorted image of Jesus to future generations, so it bequeathed huge national debts, unworkable national boundaries and unresolved racial conflicts to the countries it raped in the name of civilization. Emmanuel is civilization's unwitting victim.

It is hoped that the prayers and readings in this section will help us to make connections between Emmanuel's life and our own, for where a dichotomy exists between our worship and our world, our faith is hollow. Only when we begin to take seriously the biblical demand for justice will our prayers for peace have meaning and our faith have integrity. Such justice demands a bias towards the poor who bear the brunt of the world's wars. It recognizes that the pursuit of peace is active and dynamic, constantly engaging us in the cycle of repentance and forgiveness, reconciliation and resurrection.

—

1.  Lord, my country bleeds, raped by those who have
    removed its minerals, ravaged by entrepreneurs
    greedy for gain, exploited by rulers building
    palaces without sweat, gunned down by an army
    we don't need. Lord, heal our wounds by your
    wounds, and make us whole.

    *Chris Eddy, Sierra Leone*

2.  God of all ages and peoples,
    God of all time and beyond time,
    hear our prayers.
    Enfold us in your love as a mother embraces her child.
    Sing to us gently as a father murmurs a lullaby.
    You know our every deed, each inclination of our hearts.

    We glimpse our reflection in the healing river of
        your compassion,
    and we see with discomforting clarity our shortcomings:
    the way we hem ourselves in with hostility;
    our longing for revenge to the point
    where we obliterate hope for reconciliation;
    the old grudges carefully nurtured;
    our hearts constricted with fears.

    No, we will not give up the power of our passion for
        liberation;
    neither shall we calmly accept the collapsing of the weak
    into the will of the strong and call that reconciliation.
    Yet we know that threat begets threat,
    violence evokes violence, poisoning us all.

We have learned from our teacher and Saviour
that undeserved suffering brings its own strength,
that the route to a new life passes through death,
that a victim who stretches out her hand to another victim
casts off the victim's role,
generates a soul-force, a creative energy
that lifts both to a new vision, to new commitments,
to work for what will benefit us all.

Forgive us, O most loving Creator,
for our deafness and blindness and muteness of spirit.
Forgive us, O Life-giver, for our turning out of your voice
as it weaves its sparkling poetry through the fabric of our
   life on earth.
Forgive us the evil we have wrought, the corrosion we
have brought to the intricate and awesome sculpturing
   of your creation.
Forgive us our participation in oppression,
whether that be on the grand scale of government
or on the minor scale of home and family.

We make our confession of neglect, of corruption,
of failing to take ourselves seriously.
We confess, trusting that these uplifted prayers already
initiate the healing of all who dwell in lonely exile here.

**Lord, have mercy**
*Source unknown, Philippines*

～

3. Death has come up into our windows,
   it has entered our palaces,
   to cut off the children from the streets
   and the young men from the squares.

*Jeremiah 9:21*

4. O, the despair that wells up in me!
   O, the fear,
   the isolation,
   the loneliness.
   They mount up together
   like raging stallions,
   stampeding over me,
   crushing the life from my bones,
   bringing me to the pit of death.

   O the rage
   and the bitterness,
   the cynicism,
   the retreat into the die
   cast for those who are not strong enough
   to face the torment
   of South Africa.
   O the sweat,
   the tears,
   the dead feeling in the pit of my stomach
   at the emptiness
   that fills my being
   in the face of
   the corruption of mankind,
   the inhuman acts meted out to members
   of my race,
   the human race,
   by other members of my race,
   the human race!

   *A crisis monitor, The Natal, South Africa*

5. How wonderful it is, how pleasant,
   to be healed of the corrosive disease of racism
      and separation,
   and to live as God's people together in harmony.
   The Spirit of the Lord will then fill the hearts
   and the minds of all the people.
   Nobody will be judged any more on the basis of race or
      colour,
   but all will be ruled with justice and integrity.

   The war will end and the people together will rebuild the
      country.
   There will be no reference to the colour of the skin,
   for all will be regarded as the people of God,
   the people he created in his image.
   And this will be the beginning of what the Lord has
      promised –
   the life that never ends.

   *Psalm 133*
   *Zephania Kameeta, Namibia*

6. Standing guard without supplies.
   Night and day
   This soldier is a coward,
   Not willing to kill eye to eye
   Or one day risk
   The laughter of children
   On these polluted fields.
   A coward's war it is, where
   Sins of fathers are
   Seeded into the
   Cut of limbs
   To the third and fourth generation
   With military skill

And precision
Slicing the future
From their children's children
And yours – and mine
As well.

**Anti-personnel landmines**
*Rebecca Larsen, Germany*

7. *Leader:* Our Father who art in heaven,
   *All:* **you will that we, your children,**
   **build a new earth of sisterhood and brotherhood,**
   **not a hell of violence and death.**

   Holy be your name,
   **that in your name, Lord,**
   **there be no abuse, no oppression**
   **and no manipulation of the conscience**
   **and liberty of your children.**

   Your kingdom come,
   **not the kingdom of fear, of power, of money,**
   **of seeking peace by means of war.**

   Your will be done on earth as it is in heaven,
   **over this land of ours and other sister lands**
   **that changed their songs of joy because of oppression**
   **and the whine of the shrapnel.**

   Give us this day our daily bread,
   **the bread of peace, Lord,**
   **so that we can plant maize and beans,**
   **watch them grow**
   **and share them together as a family.**

Forgive us our sins as we forgive those who sin against us.
**May our personal and national interests
be not the coin of our exchanges.
May our laments be changed into songs of life,
clenched fists into open hands,
cries of orphans into smiles.**

Lead us not into temptation,
**the temptation of conformism, of doing nothing,
the temptation to refuse to work with you
in the search for justice and peace.**

Deliver us from evil,
**from being Cain to our brother, from being arrogant,
from believing ourselves to be lords of life and death.**

Amen.
**May it be, Lord, as you will it, according to your loving
    design.**

For yours is the kingdom and the power and the glory.
**You, Lord, are our ultimate salvation.
In you we place all our hope.**

***The Lord's Prayer***
*Refugees from El Salvador*

8. I have not yet reached the shore where there is no hatred,
   where the clouds of unjust struggles have not yet passed.
   The scars of wounds endured have not yet closed;
   warm trust in man lies totally dead.
   From the springs of forgetting I have not drunk wisdom;
   weary memories still poison me.
   From the glades of forgiveness I am still distant;
   from the sanctuary of refuge I am a great way separated.

Lord, bring me to the clear dawn of other days;
may all painful shadows depart from me.
Let me look with tender emotion on the scars of
    my wounds,
and with meek goodness upon the faces of my enemies.
Bring me to the dawn whilst the way is so long,
but do not hinder my striving until I reach the shore.

*Traian Dors, Romania*

9.  if i chant a poem and the audience
    suddenly realize
    it is they, not i, who wrote it
    then i'm praying

    when i take my place on the
    picket line and someone
    gobbs into my face and calls me
    something anglosaxon
    and i look up and see
    not an enemy
    but a different kind
    of victim
    then i'm praying...

    let my voice
    be a cobblestone
    smashing
    against a
    riotshield.

**Prayer**
*Bill Lewis, United Kingdom*

**10.** gentle breeze and piercing cold

audible silence and ear-splitting stillness

as in a screen you behold me, O God
and I behold You

I behold how You have
accompanied me
in my strivings and fallings
in my fears and awkward courage
in my eight year sojourn
in Mindanao

the cries of pain of children
women and men
refugees in their own land
driven out of their abode
by a raging war

the smell of death
of those who resist evil and tyranny

the roar of anger
of farmers and Lumads
as their land –
the source of their life –
is snatched away from them
before their very eyes

the agony of helplessness
in the face of terrifying evil

all these continue to haunt
my mind and heart even

as I savour Your presence
in this place of beauty
and bounty.

Your presence is so tangible here
I can almost touch it

and as I continue to behold You,
I was awakened
with a knife searing into flesh
that You have been with me
during these hours, and days,
and months, and years
of accompanying Your people
of Mindanao

when my eyes burned
with the searing tears
when my ribs burst with
the growing pain and hurts
when hope was blinded
with despair

I witness Your people
walking hand in hand
amidst blasts of gunfire.

**Samin from Bagio City** *(Samin stands for 'Sisters' Association
in Mindanao)*
*Ludy Panaligan, Philippines*

**11.** For the caged bird,
   for the fish on the hook,
   for the friends who are imprisoned
   because they say what they believe.

   For the uprooted flowers,
   the trampled grass,
   for the pruned trees,
   for the tortured bodies,
   I name you, Freedom.

   For the clenched teeth,
   the anger held back,
   for the knot in the throat,
   the mouths that do not sing.

   For the clandestine kiss,
   the censored poem,
   for the thousands of exiles,
   the names that cannot be spoken,
   I name you, Freedom.

   I name you in the name of everyone,
   your truc name.
   I mention you when it grows dark,
   when no one sees me.

   I write your name
   on the walls of my city,
   your true name,
   your name and other names
   that I do not name, for fear.

   For the persecuted idea,
   for the blows received,
   for the one who does not resist,
   for those who do not hide.

For the fear they have of you,
for the way they watch you,
for the way they attack you,
for the sons and daughters
that kill you,
I name you, Freedom.

*Violeta Parra, Chile*

12. Blessed Bakhita, we rejoice
at the marvels of God's love for you.

God, your divine master, raised you
from slavery to freedom,
from darkness to light,
from defeat to victory,
and through Christ, made you
one of his chosen daughters,
an honour and blessing
to our people, our country, our continent.

We ask you as Sudanese sisters and brothers
to lead us on the path of the imitation of Christ,
so that:
we may be a source of reconciliation and forgiveness,
especially in times of trials and persecution,
even praying for and loving our enemies;
we may recognize the Truth about ourselves and others,
our God-given dignity,
we may be peace-makers in our families and
communities;

we may spread the Good News of God's love
in our homes, villages and towns,
in our nation and in the world.

Blessed Bakhita, pray for us.
Amen.

*Archbishop's prayer on the occasion of the beatification
of Sister Bakhita*
*Sudan*

—

13. I dream of a community
where justice is practised
and leaders are not dictators,
where tribalism does not exist,
where leaders are honest and able,
where politicians listen in silence.
I dream of a lot more,
and I still believe God will provide.

*Clementina Naita, Kenya*

—

14. By the tender mercy of our God
the dawn from on high will
break upon us,
to give light to those who sit in
darkness and the shadow
of death
to guide our feet into the way
of peace.

*Luke 1:78–79*

# 15. LORD, WHILE THE WORLD WITH WAR AND HATRED BURNS

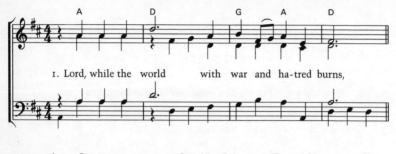

1. Lord, while the world with war and ha-tred burns,

we skim a - cross the sur-face of con - cerns,

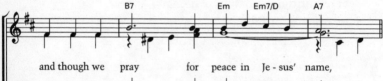

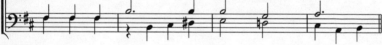

and though we pray for peace in Je - sus' name,

we lack so of - ten ur-gen - cy and shame.

Words: Fred Kaan, b. 1929. © 1989 Oxford University Press.
From *Planting Trees and Sowing Seeds*. Used by permission
Music: *Woodlands*, Walter Greatorex (1877–1949).
© Oxford University Press. Used by permission

1. Lord, while the world with war and hatred burns,
   we skim across the surface of concerns,
   and though we pray for peace in Jesus' name,
   we lack so often urgency and shame.

2. Forgive your Church its calm pursuit of peace,
   from idleness of will our lives release;
   for justice make us hungry, help us reach
   with all our passion for the good of each.

3. Speak through our voice protesting at the skill
   and science used to cripple and to kill.
   Weep with our tears, as every weapon made
   robs yet another child of human bread.

4. Cause anger, Lord, to rise within our soul,
   as all that you intended to be whole
   and full of joy is trampled underfoot
   by dint of war-machine and soldier's boot.

5. Teach us to use this anger and our will
   to sweep away the forces out to kill
   the life, the love you had of old in mind;
   we pledge our word: we are for humankind!

# 16. LA PAZ DEL SEÑOR

La paz del Se - ñor, la paz del Se - ñor, la

paz del Re - su - ci - ta - do._____

La paz del Se - ñor a ti y_a mi a

to - dos al - can - za - rá._____ - rá._____

Words and music: Anders Ruuth, v.i. tr. D. Ruffle
© 1992 the Department of Communications of ISDET, Camacua 282, 1406 Buenos Aires, Argentina
English text: Bernadette Farrell

*La paz del Señor, la paz del Señor,*
*la paz del Resucitado.*
*La paz del Señor a ti y a mi*
*a todos alcanzará.*
*La paz del Señor a ti y a mi*
*a todos alcanzará.*

1. The peace of the Lord,
   the peace of the Lord,
   the peace of the Lord Jesus Christ.
   The peace of the Lord is reaching out
   to you and to me and to all.
   The peace of the Lord is reaching out
   to you and to me and to all.

2. The peace of the Lord,
   the peace of the Lord,
   the peace of the Lord Jesus Christ.
   The peace that will heal and show the way
   is present among us today.
   The peace that will heal and show the way
   is present among us today.

3. The peace of the Lord,
   the peace of the Lord,
   the peace of the Lord Jesus Christ
   is given to you to live and share
   so that it might reach everywhere,
   is given to you to live and share
   so that it might reach everywhere.

# I7. DONA NOBIS PACEM

Dona nobis pacem, pacem.
Dona nobis pacem.
Dona nobis pacem.
Dona nobis pacem.
Dona nobis pacem.
Dona nobis pacem.

Round, traditional

# 18. THE PEACE OF GOD

The peace of God I leave you,
the peace that knows no ending,
the peace that comes when justice is done:
the peace of God for everyone.

Words and music: © 1995 Bernadette Farrell, published by ViewPoint Resources Direct,
21 Point Hill, London SE10 8QW. All rights reserved

# Work
# and Debt

Come to me all you who labour and are heavy laden and I will give you rest.

*Matthew 11:28*

~

It's hot and there are no fans. Alba has been in the factory since seven this morning. They've just raised the quota again because there's a rush order on. She's had her two-minute toilet break. She feels faint, there's no air, but she can't stop working. She's got to keep going. She's got to sew together enough T-shirts to make enough money to buy beans for her children. She hasn't felt so faint and sick since the last time she was pregnant… 'Oh no! I can't be pregnant – I'll lose my job! I've got to work, I've got to keep working – only a few more hours to go.' It'll be nine o'clock soon. Alba will be home by ten this evening, as long as she finishes her quota. Keep going, keep going, Alba.

There are millions of people like Alba, slaves to a global market that demands flexible, cheap labour. For indebted Third World countries the slogan is 'Export or die'. Whole economies, rural and urban, are geared to earning foreign currency in order to be able to maintain interest payments on their debt. Freedom for people like Alba does not exist, nor does the promised land, for they have no time even to rest, let alone dream. Their God-given right to rest – as prescribed at the world's creation – has been stripped away, and with it any regard for human dignity.

For people such as Alba the crossing of the Red Sea is a long way off. We pray we will take up Moses' challenge and work for liberation, and value people for what they are, not what they do, or how much they can produce.

~

**1.** I used to think when I was a child
that Christ might have been exaggerating when he warned
about the danger of wealth. Today I know better.
I know how very hard it is to be rich
and still keep the milk of human kindness.
Money has a dangerous way of putting scales on one's
    eyes,
a dangerous way of freezing people's hands,
eyes, lips and hearts.

*Helder Camara, Brazil*

—

**2.** The rich industrialist from the North was horrified to find
the Southern fisherman lying lazily by his boat, smoking a
pipe.

'Why aren't you out fishing?' said the industrialist.

'Because I have caught enough fish for the day,' said the
fisherman.

'Why don't you catch more than you need?' said the
industrialist.

'What would I do with it?' asked the fisherman.

'You could earn more money,' was the reply. 'With that
you could have a motor fixed to your boat. Then you could
go into deeper waters and catch more fish. Then you could
make enough money to buy nylon nets. These would
bring you more fish and more money. Soon you could have
enough money to own two boats ... maybe even a fleet of
boats. Then you could be a rich man like me.'

'What would I do then?' asked the fisherman.

'Then you could sit down and enjoy life,' said the industrialist.

'What do you think I am doing right now?' said the contented fisherman.

**The contented fisherman**
*Source unknown, Asia*

---

### 3. Don't seize control

**A.** When you make your neighbour a loan of any sort, you shall not go into his house to fetch his pledge. You shall stand outside, and the man to whom you made the loan shall bring the pledge out to you (Deuteronomy 24:10).
**B.** When you make a loan of any sort to a poor country, you shall not send in a team of experts to reorganize the economy. The people who live there shall bring proposals for change.

### There is a limit

**A.** If ever you take your neighbour's garment in pledge, you shall restore it to him before the sun goes down: for that is his only covering; it is his mantle for his body; in what else shall he sleep? (Exodus 22:26).
**B.** If ever you take interest repayments from your neighbours, you shall restore to them their dignity. There is a limit: you may not strip the poor naked.

### The means of survival

**A.** No one shall take a mill or an upper millstone in pledge; for he would be taking a life in pledge (Deuteronomy 24:6).
**B.** No one shall take the land which is used to grow corn for poor people to eat bread, and grow flowers for export instead – it is like taking people's lives in pledge.

## Protection for the poorest

**A.** When you reap your harvest in your field and have forgotten a sheaf, you shall not go back and get it: it shall be for the sojourner, and the fatherless and the widow (Deuteronomy 24:19).

**B.** When you are trying to balance your economy and you have left subsidies on basic foodstuffs, you shall not go back and remove them. They shall be for those who cannot survive without them.

## Employment

**A.** You shall not oppress a hired servant who is poor and needy. You shall give him his hire on the day he earns it, before the sun goes down (for he is poor and sets his heart upon it) (Deuteronomy 24:14).

**B.** You shall not deny a living wage to those who have only their labour to survive on. They have set their heart on it and need it today, and not in five years' time.

## Double standards

**A.** You shall not have in your bag two kinds of weight, a large and a small. A full and just weight you shall have, a full and just measure (Deuteronomy 25:13).

**B.** You shall not have in your economic theory two kinds of standard, one for the rich and the other for the poor. You shall not make poor people devalue their currency, their labour and their lives while you protect your own.

## Listen to the poor

**A.** If the poor person cries to me, I will hear, for I am compassionate (Exodus 22:27).

**B.** If the poor person cries to you, you shall hear, and be compassionate.

*The Bible and Economics*
*Janet Morley, United Kingdom*

4. Lord,
the motor under me is running hot.
Lord,
there are twenty-eight people
and lots of luggage in the truck.
Underneath are my bad tyres.
The brakes are unreliable.
Unfortunately I have no money,
and parts are difficult to get.
Lord,
'Jesus is mine'
is written on the vehicle,
for without him I would not drive a single mile.
The people in the back are relying on me.
They trust me because they see the words,
'Jesus is mine.'
Lord,
I trust you!
First comes the straight road
with little danger:
I can keep my eyes on the women,
children and chickens in the village.
But soon the road begins to turn,
it goes up and down,
it jumps and dances,
this death-road to Kumasi.
Tractors carrying mahogany trunks drive
as if there were no right or left.
Lord,
Kumasi is the temptation
to take on more people than we should.
Let's overcome it!
The road to Accra is another problem.
Truck drivers try to beat the record,
although the road is poor

and has many holes
and there are many curves
before we come to the hills.
And finally to Akwasim.
Passing large churches in every village,
I am reminded of you, and in reverence
I take off my hat.
Now down hill in second gear.

**The motor under me is running hot**
*Source unknown, Ghana*

5. You are the God of the poor,
   the simple and human God,
   the God who sweats in the street,
   the God with the weather-beaten face.

   That's why I talk to you,
   in the way that my people talk,
   because you are the labourer God,
   the worker Christ.

   **Misa Campesina**
   *Nicaragua*

6. Come, come and let us listen to the stories
   of what is happening in our times.
   Lina was a beautiful girl.
   She worked the night shift in a garment factory.
   She joined the union, participated in a mass action.
   Suddenly there was a commotion. Lina disappeared.
   Later when found, she was naked and dead.
   Come and let us cover her nakedness
   and in our hearts let Lina rest.
   Pedro Pilapil was a farmer.
   He had no other friends but the fields.
   But one day strangers came and grabbed his fields.
   Pedro protested but he was summarily killed.
   Come, come and in our hearts
   let Pedro Pilapil sow his seeds.

   Aling Maria and her family
   lived beside a garbage heap.
   One day they were bulldozed
   because tourists were coming.
   Thousands of families lost their homes.

   Come, come and let us resist
   what is happening in our times.

   *Source unknown, Philippines*

7. We raise the wheat,
   They give us the corn.
   We sift the meal,
   They give us the husk.
   We peel the meat,
   They give us the skin.
   And that's the way they take us in.

   *Slave song (1855)*

8. Perhaps if the churches had had the courage to lay the emphasis where Christ laid it, we might not have come to this present frame of mind in which it is assumed that the value of all work, and the value of all people, is to be assessed in terms of economics. We might not so readily take for granted that the production of anything (no matter how useless or dangerous) is justified so long as it issues in increased profits and wages; that so long as a man is well paid it does not matter whether his work is worthwhile in itself or good for his soul; that so long as a business deal keeps on the windy side of the law, we need not bother about its ruinous consequences to society or the individual. Or at any rate, now that we have seen the chaos of bloodshed which follows upon economic chaos, we might at least be able to listen with more confidence to the voice of an untainted and undivided Christendom.

*Dorothy L. Sayers, United Kingdom*

9. You are the God of the poor,
   The God at work in the factory.
   In your face is the wisdom of ages.
   That's why I can talk to you
   The way I talk to my friends,
   Because you are God the worker,
   And Christ is a worker too.
   You go hand in hand with all our people,
   You labour in the country and in the town.
   At the market stall you ask, 'How much?'
   Waiting for the prices to come down.
   You are in the square, laughing and singing
   With Mary and Rosa and Juan Jose.
   I have seen you standing at the corner.
   My Friend, there I called you by name.

I have seen you selling lottery tickets,
Seen you at the service station
Looking under bonnets and fixing cars,
Even filling holes along the highway
In old leather gloves and overalls.

*Source unknown, Central America*

10. *Leader:* We pray for world leaders: that they may use the power they have in the service of the poor; that they may seek opportunities to create dignified work, and enact policies which show that they believe people to be more important than profit. Lord, in your mercy,
*All:* **Hear our prayer.**

We pray for the Church: that her leaders may understand the needs and aspirations of workers and the unemployed, and that she may use her voice in their support and for their care. Lord, in your mercy,
**Hear our prayer.**

We pray for child workers, for bonded, forced and prison labourers, for all those whose work is slavery and who have no choice but to work. Let them experience the warmth of your love and compassion, particularly when it seems to them that no one cares. Lord, in your mercy,
**Hear our prayer.**

We ask that workers, employers, shareholders and consumers may understand their responsibilities and all help to build a fairer world, where the many and not just the few share in what has been created. Lord, in your mercy,
**Hear our prayer.**

**Bidding Prayers**
*Linda Jones, United Kingdom*

**11.** *All:* **We firmly believe, Lord,**
   *Leader:* that your fertile mind gave birth to all this world;
   that your artist's hand, the hand of a primitive painter,
      made beauty blossom –
   the stars and the moon, the houses and parks,
   the little boats on the river that sail down to the sea.
   And the open fields of corn, the bright yellow oil seed,
   the clumps and the woods
   sadly mutilated by the criminal axe.

   **We believe in you,**
   architect, engineer, artisan, carpenter, bricklayer, fitter.
   **We believe in you,**
   the builder of thoughts, of music and the wind, of peace
      and love.

   **We believe in you,**
   Christ the worker, light from light, the only Son of God.
   To save the world you became our flesh and blood,
   a baby in the simple and pure womb of Mary.
   We believe you were beaten, jeered at and tortured,
   then killed on the cross.
   Pilate was your judge with the authority of the law,
   stern and cruel as he washed his hands to hide his mistakes.

   **We believe in you,**
   architect, engineer, artisan, carpenter, bricklayer, fitter.
   **We believe in you,**
   the builder of thoughts, of music and the wind, of peace
      and love.

   **We believe in you,**
   comrade, the human Christ, the worker Christ.
   You overcame death, and by your enormous sacrifice
      gave birth

to a new human being who lives for freedom.
You rise from the dead with every arm that is raised
to defend the people from exploiting power.
Because you are alive in the factory,
the shops, the offices and the schools,
we believe in the struggle that you never give up,
**we believe in your resurrection.**

*Source unknown, Latin America*

12. Time in Asia was traditionally experienced as
being as unlimited as a loving mother's milk is
unlimited to her baby. Time was generously given.
It was not sold as pork chops are sold... Time was
cyclical, that is to say, calm and level-headed... It
was communal.

Now, this has been changed without any consultation
with us! ... Time is now located in the export-import
companies, motorcycle manufacturers, stores, and shops.

It is now private business property. Once it was shared,
now it is monopolized. Time does not heal us now.
Time wounds us.

***Time is money?***
*Kosuke Koyama, Asia*

13. When the tourists flew in
the Finance Minister said:
'It will boost the economy.
The dollars will flow in.'

The Minister of the Interior said:
'It will provide full and varied
employment for the indigenes.'

The Minister of Culture said:
'It will enrich our life ...
contact with other cultures
must surely improve the texture of living.'

The man from the Hilton said:
'We will make you
a second Paradise;
for you, it is the dawn
of a glorious new beginning!'

When the tourists flew in our island people
metamorphosed into
a grotesque carnival –
a two-week sideshow.

When the tourists flew in
our men put aside
their fishing nets
to become waiters;
our women became whores.

When the tourists flew in
what culture we had
flew out the window.
We traded our customs
for sunglasses and pop.
We turned sacred ceremonies
into ten-cent peep shows.

When the tourists flew in
local food became scarce.
Prices went up
but our wages stayed low.

When the tourists flew in
we could no longer
go down to our own beaches.
The hotel manager said,
'Natives defile the sea-shore.'

When the tourists flew in
the hunger and the squalor
were preserved
as a passing pageant
for clicking cameras –
a chic eyesore!

When the tourists flew in
we were asked
to be 'side-walk ambassadors',
to stay smiling and polite,
to always guide
the 'lost' visitor...
Hell, if only we could tell them
where we really want them to go!

**When the tourists flew in**
*Cecil Rajendra, Malaysia*

**14.** *Leader:* For the times when we have taken other people's work for granted,
*All:* **Lord, have mercy.**

For the times when we have paid a price lower than we could afford, because we have been more interested in paying a low price than a fair one,
**Christ, have mercy.**

For the times when we have not upheld the dignity and human rights of people in or out of work, when we have been selfish and demanding instead of compassionate and caring,
**Lord, have mercy.**

*Kyrie*
*Linda Jones, United Kingdom*

**15.** A multinational
for augmenting the domination
of a third – and even less than a third –
over the other two thirds –
and even more than two thirds –
of the human race,
reduced to a subhuman state
of wretchedness and hunger?
No.

A multinational
of faith,
of love,
of hope?
Yes!

*Hope and the multinationals*
*Helder Camara, Brazil*

# 16. SIPH'AMANDLA

Siph' - a - man - dla  N'ko - si.  Wo-kung - e - sa - bi.  Siph'-
O God, give  us  pow - er  to  rip down  pri - sons.  O

- a - man - dla  N'ko - si.  Si - ya - wa - ding - a.
God, give  us  pow - er  to  lift the  peo - ple.

Siph'amandla N'kosi. Wokungesabi.
Siph'amandla N'kosi. N'kosi Siyawadinga.

O God, give us power to rip down prisons.
O God, give us power to lift the people.

O God, give us courage to withstand hatred.
O God, give us courage not to be bitter.

O God, give us power and make us fearless.
O God, give us power because we need it.

See also material from Section 3, *The Excluded*

Words and music: from South Africa
Music arrangement: © The Iona Community. © WGRG Iona Community, Glasgow

# 17. IF YOU BELIEVE AND I BELIEVE

**Moderato**

If you be-lieve and I be-lieve and we to-geth-er

pray, ___ the Ho-ly Spi-rit must come down and

set God's peo - ple free, ___ and set God's peo - ple

free, ___ and set God's peo - ple free; ___ the

Words and music: from Zimbabwe
Music arrangement: The Iona Community.
© WGRG Iona Community, Glasgow

Ho - ly Spi - rit must come down and set God's peo - ple free.___

If you believe and I believe
and we together pray,
the Holy Spirit must come down
and set God's people free,
and set God's people free,
and set God's people free;
the Holy Spirit must come down
and set God's people free.

See also material from Section 7, *Solidarity*

# 18. IT'S NO LIFE, NO LIFE AT ALL

1. It's no life, no life at all, that's root-ed in de - cep - tion,
it's no life when hu-man warmth is miss-ing from per - cep - tion.
Liv-ing is a whole lot more than scram-bling for sur - vi - val,
go-ing through the mo-tions with your neigh-bour as a ri - val.
Je - sus Christ, he is the life, he
is the life of the world._____

Words and music: © Jaci C. Maraschin

1. It's no life, no life at all, that's rooted in deception,
   it's no life when human warmth is missing from perception.
   Living is a whole lot more than scrambling for survival,
   going through the motions with your neighbour as a rival.
   Jesus Christ, he is the life, he is the life of the world.

2. It's no life, no life at all, in slavery to suffer,
   with no shelter or a voice or money for a buffer.
   Living ought to be more like a wonderful adventure,
   with the freedom to move out in any kind of venture.
   Jesus Christ, he is the life, he is the life of the world.

3. It's no life, no life at all, when there's no future showing,
   memory is not enough to keep a person going.
   Living cannot be reliving of the past, discouraged;
   life must be attainable and real for hope to flourish.
   Jesus Christ, he is the life, he is the life of the world.

4. It is life, authentic life, that Jesus has to offer,
   working with us to transform our world where people suffer.
   Tyranny shall be no more and all oppression vanish;
   in his kingdom full of joy the fear of death is banished.
   Jesus Christ, he is the life, he is the life of the world.

# 19. LORD, YOU HAVE COME TO THE SEA-SHORE

Words: original Spanish text © 1979 Cesáreo Gabaráin, published by OCP Publications. All rights reserved.
English translation by Robert C. Trupia © 1987 OCP Publications. All rights reserved.
Music: © 1979 Cesáreo Gabaráin, arranged by Joseph Abell. Published by OCP Publications,
5536 NE Hassolo, Portland, Oregon 97213, USA. All rights reserved. Used by permission

son - ri - en - do_____ has di - cho mi
gent - ly smil - ing,_____ you have spo - ken my

nom - bre,_____ en la a - re - na_____
name;_____ all I longed for_____

_ he de - ja - do mi bar - ca,_____ jun - to a
_ I have found by the wa - ter;_____ at your

Ti_____ bus - ca - ré o - tro mar._____
side,_____ I will seek oth - er shores._____

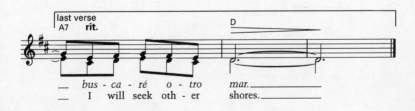

_ bus - ca - ré o - tro mar._____
_ I will seek oth - er shores._____

1. *Tú has venido a la orilla,*
   *no has buscado ni a sabios ni a ricos;*
   *tan sólo quieres que yo te siga.*

*Refrain:*
   *Señor, me has mirado a los ojos,*
   *sonriendo has dicho mi nombre,*
   *en la arena he dejado mi barca,*
   *junto a Ti buscaré otro mar.*

2. *Tú sabes bien lo que tengo;*
   *en mi barca no hay oto ni espadas,*
   *tan sólo redes y mi trabajo.*

*Refrain*

3. *Tú necesitas mis manos,*
   *mi cansancio que a otros descanse,*
   *amor que quiera seguir amando.*

*Refrain*

4. *Tú, pescador de otros lagos,*
   *ansia eterna de almas que esperan,*
   *amigo bueno, que asi me llamas.*

*Refrain*


1. Lord, you have come to the sea-shore,
   neither searching for the rich nor the wise,
   desiring only that I should follow.

*Refrain:*
   O Lord, with your eyes set upon me,
   gently smiling, you have spoken my name;
   all I longed for I have found by the water;
   at your side, I will seek other shores.

2. Lord, see my goods, my possessions,
   in my boat you find no power, no wealth.
   Will you accept, then, my nets and labour?

*Refrain*

3. Lord, take my hands and direct them.
   Help me spend myself in seeking the lost,
   returning love for the love you gave me.

*Refrain*

4. Lord, as I drift on the waters,
   be the resting place of my restless heart,
   my life's companion, my friend and refuge.

*Refrain*

# Women

She has done what lay in her power; she has anointed my body in anticipation of my burial. Truly I tell you: wherever the gospel is proclaimed throughout the world, what she has done will be told as her memorial.

*Mark 14:8–9*

~

A woman is singing, praying, digging, cleaning, sitting, staring, reading, loving, caring, fighting, dying, building, sawing, chopping, washing, planting, dreaming, despairing. She carries the hopes and dreams of others as well as her own. Her vision is of a world which is rounded and whole, where women and men share responsibility and power. A world where her work is rewarded and valued. A world where her body is respected. A world where her voice is heard and her strength is recognized. It is not just a woman's dream, it is a human dream, a dream which Christ embraced and offered to the world.

Jesus heard women when they spoke and when they were silent, when they wept and when they laughed, when they cleaned and when they listened, when they reached out and when they withdrew, when they followed him and when they anointed him, when they stood at the cross and when they announced his resurrection – and he asks us to do the same. He asks that we give value to women as well as to men, so that the human dream may find fulfilment.

The prayers and poems in this section celebrate a woman's contribution to this human dream through her work, her dignity, her suffering and her joy. Our prayer is that women and men around the globe may join the celebration, and work and dream together to build one world.

~

1. Woman of Africa
   Sweeper
   Smearing floors and waits
   With cow dung and black soil
   Cook, aya, the baby on your back
   Washer of dishes,
   Planting, weeding, harvesting
   Store-keeper, builder
   Runner of errands,
   Cart, lorry, donkey...
   Woman of Africa
   What are you not?

   *Okot p'Bitck, Uganda*

2. With Miriam, who with Moses and Aaron
   led the people of Israel out of Egypt;
   with Deborah, who judged the people of Israel
   in truth and righteousness;
   with Ruth, who was an example of faithfulness;
   with Mary Magdalen, who first
   brought the good news of the resurrection;
   with Phoebe, deacon and leader of the early Church;
   with Priscilla, who laboured with Aquila
   in the service of Christ;
   with Dorcas, who spent herself doing good
   and helping the poor;
   with Mary the mother of Jesus,
   who said 'yes' with no holding back.

   With these, our sisters,
   we pray for women everywhere who see
   their families divided,
   their children sad;
   we pray for women who against all the odds

create a good place
for their families to live in;
we pray for women who,
when tempted to give up,
find new strength from their sisters
and go on.

**For women everywhere**
B. D'Arcy, United Kingdom

3. I am a woman
    I am Filipino
    I am alive
        I am hoping

I am created in the image of God
just like all other people in the world;
I am a person with worth and dignity,
I am a thinking person, a feeling person,
a doing person.
I am the small 'I am' that stands before the big 'I AM'.

I am the worker who is constantly challenged
and faced with the needs of the Church and society
in Asia and in the global community.
I am angered by the structures and powers
that create all forms of oppression, exploitation
and degradation.

I am witness to the moans, tears, banners
and clenched fists of my people.
I can hear their liberating songs, their hopeful prayers
and decisive march toward justice and freedom.
I believe that all of us – women and men,
young and old, Christian and non-Christian –

are called upon to take responsible action;
to be concerned
to be involved
NOW!
I am hoping
  I am struggling
  I am alive
      I am Filipino
      I am a woman.

**Who am I?**
*Elizabeth Tapia, Philippines*

4. She is the Madonna of the Plains,
the woman, the mother of the dark tribes.
She holds the hands of the Son of God
and she loves us, because she is Christ's mother,
and we are Christ's brothers and sisters ...
her own beloved children in Christ.

Her eyes do not smile.
*All* things they have seen since the dream-time.
She looks over the land that was the land of our people
and our voices are known to her.

Where the little creeks murmur and the great winds
groan through the old oak trees, there she belongs.

In the night time under the stars, she is with us,
and the cries of our children touch her heart.
Her lips are curved with our pride and our pain.
Her kind hands stretch out to comfort us.
She cries for us all;
she knows all our names.
She is Mary, the great dark mother ...
the woman God loves.

She is the Madonna of the Plains.

*Patricia Mack, Australia*

5. I saw you in the doorway.
   You were black
   and bruised
   and broken.
   I knew you were someone's daughter.

   You are your mother's daughter.
   If she could,
   she would sit with you
   and say how much she loved you.

   I saw you in the shelter.
   You looked much older
   than your years.
   Your kids were tired
   and making a fuss.
   I knew you were someone's daughter.

   You are your mother's daughter.
   Imagine her here,
   as a sister and friend,
   saying how much she loves you.

   I saw you on the news last night
   on a dirt road in Soweto.
   They were screaming at you.
   You had no shoes.
   I knew you were someone's daughter.

   You are your mother's daughter,
   and she is her mother's daughter.

She has put up with so much abuse;
that shows how much she loves you.

I saw you in the delivery room
in drug withdrawal, writhing.
They say you have AIDS.
You are three hours old,
and I knew you were someone's daughter.

You are your mother's daughter
and she needs you to forgive her.
She doesn't know how to love you as yet,
but when she does,
I promise you
she will say how much she loves you.

I saw you in the orphanage.
How sad you looked
and lonely.
They say you are hard to place,
but I know you are someone's daughter.

You are your mother's daughter
and a foster mother's daughter,
and one of these days
she will come for you
and say how much she loves you.

I saw you in a nursing home.
You were slumped on a chair
with a vacant stare.
I knew you were somebody's daughter.

You are your mother's daughter,
Your Mother God's own daughter.
Soon, very soon,
She will come for you
and say how much She loves you.

**A psalm for the unloved**
*M. T. Winter, USA*

6. Daughters of Jerusalem, do not weep for me, but weep for
yourselves and for your children.

*Luke 23:28*

Jesus,
You have heard our tears:
the tears women have shed in silence
because we were afraid to be heard;
the tears women have held back
thinking we deserved violence;
the tears we have not held back
but were not comforted;
the tears women have wept alone
because we would not ask to be held;
the tears women weep together
because our sisters cannot feed their children,
because our sisters live in fear,
because the earth herself is threatened.

So we weep.

*Janet Morley, United Kingdom*

7. Sister and brother workers, we are badly abused!
   Treated like machines, despised and persecuted.
   Driven like slaves and becoming ill,
   yet all failures of the economy are blamed on us.

   Competitive power of export goods is based on low wages,
   and control of prices is based on low wages.
   When there is a slump, mass dismissal leaves us
      unemployed.
   When there is a boom, round-the-clock toiling leaves us
      weary bodies...

   Why were we born as workers? For what crime?
   Though we work our fingers to the bone,
   why can't we be free from basic hardships?
   Though we labour our whole life,
   why can't we even own a one-room house?

   When we fall ill, why can't we have
   either respite or hope of being cured?
   And when we die, why is it
   we cannot even have a proper burial?

   With prices rising at the pace of a hare,
   and wages rising at the pace of a tortoise,
   in times of illness, ten years' savings
   can disappear in a flash.
   Life for the worker is suffering one loss after another.

   **Women industrial workers**
   *Anon., Korea*

**8.** I believe in God, our mother all powerful,
Creator of heaven and earth,
Creator of woman in her own image and likeness.

I believe in God, father and mother,
bearer of forgiveness and tenderness,
strength and hope
for all the world's poor.

I believe in the Word and the strength of life
which exist and have existed in God
since the beginning of life.

I believe in Christian women of the people
who have become aware and are organizing
for solidarity and in defence of life.

I believe in the women for whom the defence of life
is the ultimate end and justification for the struggle.

I believe in woman as the living symbol of the people,
a woman who does not subject herself to the oppressor
because she will never give up her faith,
her culture or her identity.

I believe in woman who generates life,
who is strength and a catalyst for change.

I believe in the Church of the poor
and its potential for holiness and understanding,
a Church capable of making the faith of the people
human, democratic and unified.

*Pastoral Andina*
*Peru*

9. Your feet tell the toll
   Of a life's stroll

   To and from the bush
   With wood on your head

   To and from the farm
   To till the land
   With nothing under your feet.

   Your feet cracking
   Like a drying dam crumbling
   Are living proof.

   **Old African women**
   *Source unknown, Africa*

10. For the Mighty God has done great things for me.
    His name is Holy,
    his mercy sure from generation to generation
    to those who fear him.
    He has shown the might of his arm,
    he has routed the proud and all their schemes;
    he has brought down the monarchs from their thrones,
    and raised on high the lowly.
    He has filled the hungry with good things,
    and sent the rich away empty.

    **The Magnificat**
    *Luke 1:49–53*

# II. STAND, O STAND FIRM

**Confidently**

**All:** Stand, O stand firm; stand, O stand firm; stand, O stand firm and see what the Lord can do.

**Cantor:** O my sisters, stand very firm!

**All:**
Stand, O stand firm;
stand, O stand firm;
stand, O stand firm
and see what the Lord can do.

**Cantor:**
O my sisters, stand very firm!

**All:**
Stand, O stand firm;
stand, O stand firm;
stand, O stand firm
and see what the Lord can do.

**Cantor:** (Other verses ad lib.)

Words: traditional, Cameroons
Music: origin unknown
Arrangement © 1990 The Iona Community. © WGRG Iona Community, Glasgow

# 12. WOMEN SPEAK JUSTICE

Words and music: Helen Kearins, RSM © 1991, Sisters of Mercy,
PO Box 221, Goulburn, NSW 2580, Australia

1. A woman with hem'rhage, an outcast,
   through the crowd touches his cloak.
   Her sisters in cities and churches
   pour life-blood, still breaking the yoke.

*Refrain:*
   And there's no more walking in silence,
   no more living in fear,
   women speaking justice;
   listen who have ears to hear.

2. She had a bad name in the city,
   with ointment she covered his feet.
   To those who preach law, not encounter,
   compassion and laughter we mete.

*Refrain*

3. A woman maligned and abandoned
   draws water, then enters debate.
   Our wells and our stories we treasure,
   refusing to be second-rate.

*Refrain*

4. Martha, concerned for appearance,
   Mary, content to be free.
   Too many things in our cupboards.
   Women beginning to see.

*Refrain*

5. She runs to his tomb in the morning,
   proclaims that he's risen today.
   Concerned for the earth and her people,
   such women will not go away.

*Refrain*

See also material from Section 3, *The Excluded*

# 13. ENEMY OF APATHY

Words: The Iona Community. © WGRG Iona Community, Glasgow
Music: John L. Bell, The Iona Community. © WGRG Iona Community, Glasgow

1. She sits like a bird, brooding on the waters,
   hovering on the chaos of the world's first day;
   she sighs and she sings, mothering creation,
   waiting to give birth to all the Word will say.

2. She wings over the earth, resting where she wishes,
   lighting close at hand or soaring through the skies;
   she nests in the womb, welcoming each wonder,
   nourishing potential hidden to our eyes.

3. She dances in fire, startling her spectators,
   waking tongues of ecstasy where dumbness reigned;
   she weans and inspires all whose hearts are open,
   nor can she be captured, silenced or restrained.

4. For she is the Spirit, one with God in essence,
   gifted by the Saviour in eternal love;
   she is the key opening the scriptures,
   enemy of apathy and heavenly dove.

See also material from Section 1, *Environment and Land*

# Solidarity

So if I, your Lord and Teacher, have washed your feet, you also
ought to wash one another's feet.

*John 13:14*

~

The Bible gives us many examples of people who were united
often in difficult and dangerous circumstances: the people of
the Exodus and the Exile come together in their struggle; Ruth
and Naomi support each other in their grief; and Ebimelech
risks his own life to save the much maligned Jeremiah. But
more than any other person, it is Jesus who shows us the
meaning of the word 'solidarity'. Jesus came to be one of us,
to stand alongside us and to suffer with us.

As his disciples, we too are called to stand alongside the poor
and journey with them, to listen to their voice and plead their
cause. Should we need encouragement, we need look no
further than the developing world for inspiration.

Small co-operatives thrive in the Third World, their members
committed to each other in their determination to make a
living. In war-torn countries women support each other in the
absence of their menfolk, united in their bid for survival by
mutual compassion. In Brazil, homeless families come together
to occupy unused land, boldly defying the power wielded by
millionaire landowners. In countries such as Bangladesh,
exploited factory workers, under threat of violence, stand
together to form unions in an effort to protect their rights.

This struggle of the poor to hold on to life in fellowship with
each other is not only expressed in their daily life and work,
but also in their worship, songs and dances. By putting our lips
to their words – whether they are from the shanty towns of
Brazil, the tea plantations of Sri Lanka, or the townships of
South Africa – we are not only enriching our own worship and

our understanding of fellowship, but also expressing solidarity
with them. We pray that our actions will reflect our prayers.

1.  You asked for my hands
    that you might use them for your purpose.
    I gave them for a moment,
    then withdrew them, for the work was hard.

    You asked for my mouth
    to speak out against injustice;
    I gave you a whisper that I might not be accused.

    You asked for my eyes
    to see the pain of poverty;
    I closed them, for I did not want to see.

    You asked for my life
    that you might work through me.
    I gave a small part, that I might not get 'too involved'.

    Lord, forgive me for my calculated efforts to serve you
    only when it is convenient for me to do so,
    only in those places where it is safe to do so and
    only with those who make it easy to do so.

    Father, forgive me,
    renew me,
    send me out
    as a usable instrument
    that I might take seriously
    the meaning of your cross.

*A prayer from Africa*
*Joe Seremane, South Africa*

2. An ancient Rabbi once asked his pupils how they could
   tell when the night had ended and the day was on its
   way back.

   'Could it be,' asked one student, 'when you can see an
   animal in the distance and tell whether it is a sheep
   or a dog?'

   'No,' answered the Rabbi.

   'Could it be,' asked another, 'when you can look at a tree
   in the distance and tell whether it is a fig tree or a
   peach tree?'

   'No,' said the Rabbi.

   'Well then, what is it?' his pupils demanded.

   'It is when you look on the face of any woman or man
   and see that she or he is your sister or brother. Because if
   you cannot do this, then, no matter what time it is, it is
   still night.'

   **Old Jewish Story**
   *Source unknown*

3. We talk of 'living in Christ with people' – what people?
   We have torn ourselves apart from the rest of our body.
   Lest you turn aside from us,
   we reach out our hands to grasp our severed limbs,
   we reach out to the unloved, the unwashed, the ulcerated.
   We reach out to those imprisoned: imprisoned behind bars,
   imprisoned behind masks, imprisoned in endless labour.

We reach out to those who sell their bodies for money;
or sell their children for money;
or sell their country for money.
With reluctance we reach out to those who crucify us,
the powerful, the oppressors, the rich.
Come, bone of our bones, flesh of our flesh,
join with us, making us whole again!
Spirit of the living God, come,
put breath in us and bring us to life,
cleanse us, renew us, empower us.
In the name of Christ, in whom alone we are complete.

**Presence**
*Christian conference, Asia*

⚊

4. When spiders unite they can tie up a lion.

*Ethiopian proverb*

⚊

5. Don't moralize
or marginalize,
open wide your door.
Don't sympathize –
empathize,
live beside the poor.
Don't despise
or close your eyes,
put yourself in our place.
Listen, learn,
and realize
we are all one human race.

**True partnership**
*Moraene Roberts, United Kingdom*

6. Lord, is it not possible today completely
   to live out your gospel?
   Are we not able to live in unity
   nor to have things in common?
   When will we sell our possessions
   to share them among all people,
   according to the need of each other?
   What are we waiting for
   before praying together
   and in silence?
   To become united in the same Spirit,
   to break bread in our families,
   and to take this food happily,
   being simple of heart,
   and only praising the Lord?
   Or have you asked the impossible of us,
   since not everyone loves us?

   *Fermin Cebello Lopez, Nicaragua*

7. We cannot know whether we love God, although there
   may be strong reasons for thinking so, but there can be no
   doubt whether we love our neighbour or no.

   *St Teresa of Avila*

8. On the night before his death, Jesus takes a piece of bread,
   breaks it and says, 'This is my body given for you. Do this
   in my memory.' To do this in his memory is not primarily
   about repeating a ritual memorial service, but is about
   allowing his Spirit so to possess us that we see our lives as

bread to be broken that others may live. This is to share in God's own life, expressed uniquely in Jesus.

*Gerard Hughes, United Kingdom*

9. *Leader:*
Come, Lord,
do not smile and say
you are already with us.
Millions do not know you,
and to us who do,
what is the difference?
What is the point of your presence
if our lives do not alter?

*All:*
**Change our lives,
shatter our complacency.
Make your word
flesh of our flesh,
blood of our blood
and our life's purpose.
Take away the quietness
of a clear conscience.
Press us uncomfortably,
for only thus
that other peace is made –
Your peace.**

*Helder Camara, Brazil*

10. We shall have to repent in this generation, not so much
for the evil deeds of the wicked people, but the appalling
silence of the good people.

*Martin Luther King, USA.*

11. Compassionate God,
open our hearts
that we may feel the breath and play of your Spirit,
unclench our hands
that we may reach out to one another in openness and
generosity,
free our lips
that we may speak for those whose voices are not heard,
unblock our ears
to hear the cries of the broken-hearted,
and open our eyes
to see Christ in friend and stranger,
that in sharing our love and our pain,
our poverty and our prosperity,
we may move towards that peace and justice which comes
from you
and so be bearers of divine reconciliation.
Amen.

*Annabel Shilson-Thomas, United Kingdom*

12. My God, I need to have signs of your grace.
Serve me your sacraments,
the first fruits of your kingdom.
I thirst for smiles,
for sweet odours,
for soft words,

for firm gestures,
for truth and goodness,
and for triumphs
(no matter how small)
of justice.

You know, O God, how hard it is to survive captivity
without any hope of the Holy City.
Sing to us, God, the songs of the promised land.
Serve us your manna in the desert.
Let there be, in some place,
a community of men, women, elderly,
children, and new-born babies
as a first fruit,
as our appetizer,
and our embrace of the future. Amen.

*Rubem Alves, Brazil*

13. Lord of all creation, we stand in awe before you, impelled
by the visions of harmony of humankind. We are children
of many traditions – inheritors of shared wisdom and
tragic misunderstandings, of proud hopes and humble
successes. Now it is time for us to meet – in memory and
truth, in courage and trust, in love and promise.

In that which we share, let us see the common prayer for
humanity; in that which we differ, let us wonder at the
freedom of humankind; in our unity and our differences,
let us know the uniqueness that is God.

May our courage match our convictions, and our integrity
match our hope.

May our faith in You bring us closer to each other.

May our meeting with past and present bring blessing for
the future. Amen.

**Prayer for inter-faith meetings**
*The Association of Rabbis of the Reform Synagogue
of Great Britain, United Kingdom*

14. *Leader:* Our God, who art in heaven, hallowed be
your name in peoples across the world, of different
races, colours and religions; single people, couples
and families; people at work or out of work, at home
or homeless.
*All:* **May your kingdom come.**

May your kingdom come and your will be done on earth,
in the ways in which we act, the choices which we make,
the action for change which we take and which we
encourage in others.
**May your kingdom come.**

Give us this day our daily bread: bread which we work for,
food which we share, bread which no one should be denied
because of the greed of others.
**May your kingdom come.**

Forgive us our trespasses: times when we have condemned
instead of being constructive; times when we have not
listened but only preached; times when we have failed to
do what we know we should have done; times when we
have not shown compassion and forgiveness.
**May your kingdom come.**

Lead us not into temptation: temptation to close our
minds, our ears and our eyes to reality; temptation to be
afraid to speak out against injustice; temptation to think

it's all too much and that what we do won't make any
difference; temptation to think that there is
no alternative.
**May your kingdom come.**

Deliver us from evil: the evil of a world where people
don't count; the evil of powerlessness and loss of hope; the
evil of a world where gates, walls and barriers between
people grow ever higher; the evil of a world where money
is more important than people and where the last debt
repayment must be squeezed out of the South, no matter
what the human cost.
**May your kingdom come, for yours is the kingdom, the
power and the glory for ever and ever. Amen.**

*Linda Jones (adapted), United Kingdom*

15. God, our guide,
    we live in hope for the future;
    we are determined to go on,
    to venture with the help of our partners,
    making a great effort,
    so that 'those who were no people'
    may become truly your people.
    Difficult days lie ahead,
    but we believe that in the end,
    with your help,
    we shall overcome.

    ***A prayer for Haiti***
    *Alain Rocourt, Haiti*

**16.** I believe in the equality of all,
rich and poor.
I believe in liberty.
I believe in humanity through which
we can create unity.
I believe in the love within each of us,
and in the home, happy and healthy.
I believe in the forgiveness of our sins.
I believe that with divine help
we will have the strength to establish
equality in society.
I believe in unity, the only way to
achieve peace, and I believe that
together we can obtain justice.

*Young people of Ayacucho, Peru*

**17.** God, help us to change.
To change ourselves
and to change our world.
To know the need for it.
To deal with the pain of it.
To feel the joy of it.
To undertake the journey without understanding the
    destination.
The art of gentle revolution.

*Leuing, Australia*

# 18. THE SERVANT SONG

1. Will you let me be your ser-vant,

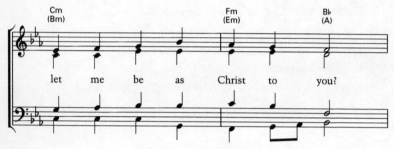

let me be as Christ to you?

Pray that I may have the grace to

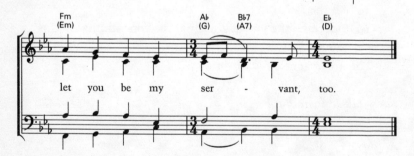

let you be my ser - vant, too.

*Guitar chords and vocal harmonies are not compatible.

Words and music: Richard Gillard. Music arrangement by Betty Pulkingham (b. 1929).
© 1977 Scripture in Song, administered by Kingsway's Thankyou Music,
PO Box 75, Eastbourne, East Sussex BN23 6NW, UK. Used by permission

1. Will you let me be your servant,
   let me be as Christ to you?
   Pray that I may have the grace to
   let you be my servant, too.

2. We are pilgrims on a journey,
   we are travellers on the road;
   we are here to help each other,
   walk the mile and bear the load.

3. I will hold the Christ-light for you
   in the night-time of your fear;
   I will hold my hand out to you,
   speak the peace you long to hear.

4. I will weep when you are weeping;
   when you laugh I'll laugh with you.
   I will share your joy and sorrow
   'til we've seen this journey through.

5. When we sing to God in heaven
   we shall find such harmony,
   born of all we've known together
   of Christ's love and agony.

6. Will you let me be your servant,
   let me be as Christ to you?
   Pray that I may have the grace to
   let you be my servant, too.

# 19. JESU, JESU, FILL US WITH YOUR LOVE

Je - su,_____ Je - su,_____ fill us with your love, show us how to serve the neigh - bours we have from you.

1. Kneels at the feet of his friends, si - lent - ly wash - es their feet, Mas - ter who pours out him - self_____ for them._____

Words: Ghanaian folk song based on John 13:3–5 translated by Tom Colvin (b. 1925)
Music: *Chereponi* (Ghanaian folk melody), adapted by Tom Colvin;
arranged by Jane Marshall (b. 1924), © 1969, 1982, Hope Publishing Company,
administered by CopyCare Ltd, PO Box 77, Hailsham, East Sussex BN27 3EF, UK. Used by permission

*Refrain:*
    Jesu, Jesu, fill us with your love,
    show us how to serve
    the neighbours we have from you.

1. Kneels at the feet of his friends,
   silently washes their feet,
   Master who pours out himself for them.

*Refrain*

2. Neighbours are rich and poor,
   neighbours are black and white,
   neighbours are near and far away.

*Refrain*

3. These are the ones we should serve,
   these are the ones we should love.
   All are neighbours to us and you.

*Refrain*

4. Kneel at the feet of our friends,
   silently washing their feet,
   this is the way we should live with you.

*Refrain*

# 20. SENT BY THE LORD AM I

Words: from the oral tradition. Translation © 1991 Jorge Maldonado
Music: Traditional Nicaraguan melody

task is mine to do, to set it real - ly free. Oh,

help me to o - bey; help me to do your will.

Sent by the Lord am I;
my hands are ready now
to make the earth the place
in which the kingdom comes.
Sent by the Lord am I;
my hands are ready now
to make the earth the place
in which the kingdom comes.

The angels cannot change
a world of hurt and pain
into a world of love,
of justice and of peace.
The task is mine to do,
to set it really free.
Oh, help me to obey;
help me to do your will.

# 21. WHO WILL SPEAK

Who will speak* if we/you don't?
Who will speak if we/you don't?
Who will speak so their voice will be heard?
Oh, who will speak if we/you don't?

(*Alternatives: 'work', 'care'.)

Words and music: Marty Haugen, adapted from a homily by Ray East.
© 1993 GIA Publications Inc. All rights reserved. A full harmony version with verses is also available.

# Celebrating
## Hope

Then shall the young women
rejoice in the dance,
and the young men and the old
shall be merry.
I will turn their mourning into joy.
I will comfort them, and give them gladness for sorrow.

*Jeremiah 31:13*

⁓

The belief that we are called to establish God's kingdom of
justice and peace here on earth is a vital part of Christian hope
for the future. God's people are inspired by a vision of a
kingdom in which all are valued as being made in the image of
their Creator. It is a vision shared by the prophets of old, and
one which Jesus himself honoured:

he has sent me to announce good news to the poor,
to proclaim release for prisoners and recovery of sight for
    the blind;
to let the broken victims go free,
to proclaim the year of the Lord's favour (Luke 4:18–19).

As Christ's hands and feet on earth, we are not just called to
dream, but to make our dream a reality. Whenever we are in
danger of losing sight of God's vision, the poor of our world
point us in the direction of their dreams. They continue to
hope against hope, for hopelessness is a luxury they
cannot afford.

This determination to hold on to hope and embrace all that is
precious, coupled with a commitment to work for change and
to turn from death to life, frequently finds expression in the
energy and enthusiasm of their worship. Let us join with them
and celebrate the hope that together we can change our
present and inaugurate God's future.

1. Creator God,
   we announce your goodness because
   it is clearly visible in the heavens,
   where there is the light of the sun,
   the heat of the sun,
   and the light of night.
   There are rain clouds.

   The land itself shows your goodness,
   because it can be seen
   in the trees and their shade.
   It is clearly seen in water and grass,
   in the milking cows and in the cows that give us meat.

   Your love is visible all the time:
   morning and daytime, evening and night.
   Your love is great.
   It has filled the land; it has filled people.

   We say 'Thank you, our God',
   because you have given us everything we have.
   You have given us our fathers and mothers,
   our brothers and sisters, our friends.

   We have nothing except what you have given us.
   You are our shield; you protect us.
   Your are our guard; you take care of us.
   You are our safety, all days.

   You stay with us for ever and ever.
   You are our father and mother.
   Therefore we say: 'Thank you.'

We worship you with our mouths.
We worship you with our bodies.
We worship you with everything we have
because only you have given us everything.

We say: 'Thank you' today.
And tomorrow. And all days.
We do not tire in giving thanks to you.

*A Masai prayer, Kenya*

2. O God of all youth, we pray to you:
   we are young people, and we want to celebrate life!
   We cry out against all that kills life:
   hunger, poverty, unemployment, sickness, repression,
   individualism, injustice.
   We want to announce fullness of life:
   work, education, health, housing, bread for all.
   We want communion, a world renewed.
   We hope against hope.
   With the Lord of history we want to make all things new.

   *A youth group, Brazil*

3. Stand up and look at the mountain,
   source of the sun, of water and the wind.
   You can harness the rush of mighty rivers,
   you who gather the harvest of our soul.
   Stand up and look at your own hands,
   reach out to hold your brother's hand in your hand.
   Together we will go forward, united by blood,
   knowing the future can be now.
   Deliver us from the oppression which keeps us in poverty.

Lead us into your kingdom of justice and equality.
Let your will be done here on earth.
Give us your strength and courage in the struggle.
Stand up and look at our land,
reach out your hand to your sister.
Together we go forward, united by our death.

*Victor Jara, Chile*

4. When the heart is hard and parched up,
   come upon me with a shower of mercy.
   When grace is lost from life,
   come with a burst of song.
   When tumultuous work raises its din,
   shutting me out from beyond,
   come to me, my Lord of silence,
   with thy peace and rest.
   When my beggarly heart sits crouched,
   shut up in a corner,
   break open the door, my King,
   and come with the ceremony of a king.
   When desire blinds the mind with delusion and dust,
   O thou holy one, thou wakeful,
   come with thy light and thy thunder.

*Rabindranath Tagore, Bangladesh*

5. I am a youth.
   There are many dreams I have had,
   many fantasy dreams I had made,
   many I had reached,
   many I have to await.
   A nightmare came so suddenly,

no time for me to think but run.
In a foreign land,
I sat on the top of the hill and looked
at the direction from where I came.
I buried my head in my hands,
cried for Rwanda, my sweet motherland.
I am a refugee.
I have lost my homeland.
As days went by,
I realized the nightmare had broken
my dreams into a thousand pieces.
That made me afraid.
I am afraid to see the broken dreams,
I am afraid to dream again.
I do not know how to put
the broken dreams together,
I do not know how to dream again.

I am a refugee, but I am a youth.
Isn't it the nature to have dreams
for our lives?
How can life go on without a dream?
I am a refugee, but I am a youth.
Affirmation of my identity
is what I need.
I am a refugee, but I am a youth.
I want to see my spirit on fire.
Let it burst into flame,
to continue my dreams,
to keep my hopes alive.
I painfully wait,
struggling for transformation.
Oh friend, open your arm,
give me your hand.
With heart of compassion
we can start to understand.
Support my dreams,

strengthen my struggles,
reach out your hand
across the land.
*'Urakoze'* is the word of thanks I say,
*'Amarahoro'* is God's peace for you, I pray.

*Uwimana Uwamaholo Le Kheng (1995), Rwanda*

⁓

6. I'm my mother's eldest son. I had a little brother,
   but he was hit by a bullet during the fighting and
   he died. Now I'm all alone. My mother was
   already an invalid and she was killed by UNITA.

If you go up to someone's house, they call you a
thief. And I am not a thief. But even if you are not a thief
they accuse you of being one. Many people call us street
urchins, walking the streets in dirty clothes and begging.

Some people say, 'Look at this vermin.' And I say,
'You know nothing. What are you talking about?'
And I walk away.

Sometimes you meet people who hit you and I say, 'What
have I done?' But that makes them even angrier. And they
start beating you again. You have to keep quiet. You're
hurt and only God knows about it. That's how it is. I hope
someone can take me away from the airport. Even if it's
just for a weekend. I wouldn't have to sleep in the streets
and be killed by bandits.

I think about a lot of things. I'd like to live in a house and
be free. I'd like to live somewhere where I wouldn't have
to fight with others. Where I could play with my friends.
Where I could have a bath, wander around, watch TV.
And after watching TV then go and play. Then go to sleep

and next day, play again. Do the washing up and clean the
house. And after that, I'd play on the veranda with my
very own toys. That's what I'd like...

*Domingo Claudio, aged 10, Angola*

—

7. The wolf shall dwell with the lamb,
   and the leopard shall lie down with the kid,
   and the calf and the lion and the fatling together,
   and a child shall lead them.
   The cow and the bear shall feed;
   their young shall lie down together;
   and the lion shall eat straw like the ox.
   The sucking child shall play over the hole of the asp,
   and the weaned child shall put his hand on the adder's den.
   They shall not hurt or destroy in all my holy mountain;
   for the earth shall be full of the knowledge of the Lord
   as the waters cover the sea.

*Isaiah 11:6–9*

—

8. I, sinner and bishop, confess to arriving in Rome
   with my rural crook,
   taking the colonnades by surprise
   and practising my panpipes to drown out the sound of the
       organ;
   to having arrived in Assisi, circled about by poppies.
   I, sinner and bishop, confess to dreaming of a Church
   clothed only in the Gospel and sandals;
   to believing in the Church,
   sometimes even in spite of the Church;
   to believing in the Kingdom
   in any case, walking in the Church.

I, sinner and bishop, confess to having seen Jesus of
    Nazareth
announcing the Good News to the poor of Latin America;
to saying to Mary 'Hail, mother and friend of all!';
to celebrating the blood of those who have been faithful;
to being a pilgrim.
I, sinner and bishop, confess to loving Nicaragua, a child
    of the times.
I, sinner and bishop, confess to opening the window of
    time every morning;
to speaking to others like brother to brother;
to never losing my dream, my song, my laugh;
to cultivating the flower of hope amid the wounds of the
    Risen One.

***I, sinner and bishop, confess***
*Pedro Casaldaliga (translated by Linda Jones), Nicaragua*

9. O God, our loving and Eternal Parent, we praise you with
   a great shout of joy! Your ruling power has proved
   victorious! For centuries our land seemed too dark for
   sunrise, too bloody for healing, too sick for recovery, too
   hateful for reconciliation. But you have brought us into
   the daylight of liberation; you have healed us with new
   hope; you have stirred us to believe our nation can be
   reborn; we see the eyes of our sisters and brothers shining
   with resolve to build a new South Africa. Accept our
   prayers of praise and thanksgiving.

   We thank you for the spiritual power which gives us new
   birth. You have given us courage to change our minds, to
   open our hearts to those we despised, and to discover we
   can disagree without being enemies. We are not winners
   and losers but citizens who push and pull together to
   move the nation forward. We thank you for the Good

News that you will always be with us, and will always
overcome: that love will conquer hatred; that tolerance
will conquer antagonism; that co-operation will conquer
conflict; that your Holy Spirit can empower our spirits;
through Jesus Christ our Lord.

***Our loving and Eternal Parent***
*National Service of Thanksgiving, May 1994, South Africa*

10. Our Father,
    who is in us here on earth,
    holy is your name
    in the hungry who share their bread and their song.
    Your kingdom come,
    a generous land where confidence and truth reign.
    Let us do your will,
    being a cool breeze for those who sweat.
    You are giving us our daily bread
    when we manage to get back our lands
    or to get a fairer wage.
    Forgive us
    for keeping silent in the face of injustice
    and for burying our dreams.
    Don't let us fall into the temptation
    of taking up the same arms as the enemy,
    but deliver us from the evil which disunites us.
    And we shall have believed in humanity and in life
    and we shall have known your kingdom
    which is being built for ever and ever.

***Lord's Prayer***
*Central America*

**11.** How lonely I am in the unknown world,
far from my wife and children.
Throughout all the time I always wonder
whether I am lost or forgotten by my God who created me
to live under the evils of this world.
Oh children, my children, be good to your mother,
be humble under the good examples you are shown.
If I had wings I could just fly back home
to rest under the shadow of my peach tree
to forget these hardships.

*A migrant worker, South Africa*

**12.** God who listens and hears when we pray,
we know that you are with us on our journey through life;
you have told us that you are with us always.
Help us to believe in a more just world.
Help us to dream a new vision.
Give us the openness to work with others to make
a difference.
Hold us up when we stumble, when there are obstacles
and we don't know the way forward.
Give us the confidence to challenge injustice,
and to nurture the flame of justice until it burns brightly.

And may the Spirit of justice and community
accompany you throughout your life.

May this Spirit move you, heal you,
guide you and challenge you;
call you to action and to prayer.

May a passion for justice burn through you and in you,
and may it warm the hearts of those around you,
encouraging hope and overcoming fear.

**Prayer and blessing**
*Linda Jones, United Kingdom*

13. Our culture has taught, let time follow its natural
course – like the seasons. We watch the moon in
each of its phases. We wait for the rain to fill our
rivers and water the thirsty earth. When twilight
comes, we prepare for night. At dawn we rise
with the sun.

We watch the bush foods grow and wait for them to ripen
before we gather them. We wait for our young people to
grow stage by stage through their initiation ceremonies.
When a relation dies we wait a long time with the sorrow.
We own our grief and allow it to heal slowly.

We don't like to hurry. There is nothing more important
than what we are attending to. There is nothing more
urgent we must hurry away for.

We wait on God too. His time is the right time. We wait
for him to make his word clear to us. We don't worry. We
know that in time and in the spirit of deep listening and
quiet stillness his way will be made clear.

**The Aboriginal gift**
*Miriam Rose Ungunmerr, Australia*

**14.** Live slowly, think slowly, for time is a mystery.
Never forget that love requires always that you be
the greatest person you are capable of being.

Be grateful for the manifold
dreams of creation
and the many ways of the unnumbered peoples.

Be grateful for life as you live it
and may a wonderful light
always guide you on the unfolding road.

From ***A Benediction to an English friend in Africa***
*Ben Okri, Nigeria*

# 15. GLORIA, GLORIA

Glo - ria, glo - ria, glo - ria / en las al - tur - as a Dios!
Glo - ry, glo - ry, glo - ry, / glo - ry be to God on high!

Y en la tie - rra paz pa - ra aque-llos / que a-ma el Se - ñor.___
And on earth_ peace to the peo - ple in whom God is well pleased.

Gloria, gloria, gloria
en las alturas a Dios!
Gloria, gloria, gloria
en las alturas a Dios!
Y en la tierra paz para aquellos
que ama el Señor.
Y en la tierra paz para aquellos
que ama el Señor.

Glory, glory, glory,
glory be to God on high!
Glory, glory, glory,
glory be to God on high!
And on earth peace to the people
in whom God is well pleased.
And on earth peace to the people
in whom God is well pleased.

Words: Luke 2:14
Music: © Pablo D. Sosa

# 16. SIYAHAMBA
## (WE ARE MARCHING)

Words: Traditional South African chant, collected and edited by Anders Nyberg.
© WGRG Iona Community, Glasgow
Music: African melody scored by Notman KB, Ljungsbro and Lars Parkman.
Arrangement by The Iona Community. © WGRG Iona Community, Glasgow

Siyahamb' ekukhanyen' kwenkhos',
siyahamb' ekukhanyen' kwenkhos'.
Siyahamb' ekukhanyen' kwenkhos',
siyahamb' ekukhanyen' kwenkhos'.
Siyahamba, Oo
Siyahamb' ekukhanyen' kwenkhos'.
Siyahamba, Oo
Siyahamb' ekukhanyen' kwenkhos'.

We are marching in the light of God,
we are marching in the light of God,
we are marching in the light of God,
we are marching in the light of God.
We are marching, Oo,
we are marching in the light of God.
We are marching, Oo,
We are marching in the light of God.

# 17. CITY OF GOD

1. A-wake from your slum-ber!_ A - rise from your sleep! A new day is dawn-ing_ The peo-ple in dark-ness_ have seen a great light. The Lord of our long-ing_ has con-quered the night._

2. We are sons of the morn-ing;_ we are daugh-ters of day. The one who has loved us_ has bright-ened our way. The Lord of all kind-ness_ has called us to be a light for his peo-ple_ to set their hearts free._

Based on Isaiah 9:60; 1 John 1

Words and music: © 1977 Daniel Schutte and New Dawn Music Inc.
Published by OCP Publications, 5536 NE Hassolo, Portland, Oregon 97213, USA.
All rights reserved. Used by permission

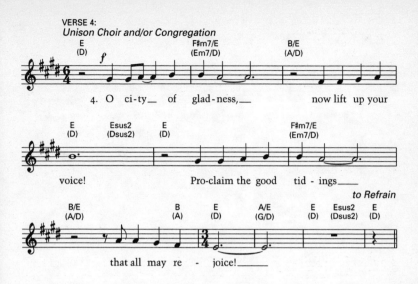

**VERSE 4:**
*Unison Choir and/or Congregation*

4. O ci-ty__ of glad-ness,__ now lift up your voice! Pro-claim the good tid - ings__

*to Refrain*

that all may re - joice!_____

1. Awake from your slumber! Arise from your sleep!
   A new day is dawning for all those who weep.
   The people in darkness have seen a great light.
   The Lord of our longing has conquered the night.

*Refrain:*
   Let us build the city of God.
   May our tears be turned into dancing!
   For the Lord, our light and our love,
   has turned the night into day!

2. We are sons of the morning; we are daughters of day.
   The one who has loved us has brightened our way.
   The Lord of all kindness has called us to be
   a light for his people to set their hearts free.

*Refrain*

3. God is light; in him there is no darkness.
   Let us walk in his light, his children, one and all.
   O comfort my people; make gentle your words.
   Proclaim to my city the day of her birth.

*Refrain*

4. O city of gladness, now lift up your voice!
   Proclaim the good tidings that all may rejoice!

*Refrain*

# 18. WE HAVE HOPE / TENEMOS ESPERANZA

1. Be-cause he came in-to our world and sto-ry, be-cause he heard our sil-ence and our sor-row, be-cause he filled the whole world with his glo-ry, and came to light the dark-ness of our mor-row, be-cause his birth was in a dark-ened cor-ner, be-cause he lived pro-claim-ing life and love,___ be-cause he quick-ened hearts that had been dor-mant, and lift-ed those whose lives had been down-trod-den. So

Words: Federico J. Pagura
Music: Homero Ferara

1. Because he came into our world and story,
   because he heard our silence and our sorrow,
   because he filled the whole world with his glory,
   and came to light the darkness of our morrow,
   because his birth was in a darkened corner,
   because he lived proclaiming life and love,
   because he quickened hearts that had been dormant,
   and lifted those whose lives had been downtrodden.

*Refrain:*
   So we today have hope and expectation.
   So we today can struggle with conviction.
   So we today can trust we have a future,
   so we have hope (in this our world of tears).
   So we today have hope and expectation.
   So we today can struggle with conviction.
   So we today can trust we have a future,
   so we have hope.

2. Because he drove the merchants from the temple,
   denouncing evil and hypocrisy,
   because he raised up little ones and women,
   and put down all the mighty from their seats,
   because he bore the cross for our wrongdoings,
   and understood our failing and our weakness,
   because he suffered from our condemnation
   and then he died for every mortal creature.

*Refrain*

3. Because of victory one morning early,
   when he defeated death and fear and sorrow,
   so nothing can hold back his mighty story
   nor his eternal kingdom tomorrow.

*Refrain*

*The first half of verse 3 may be hummed or instrumental, voices entering at measure 8.

# 19. WE SHALL GO OUT
# WITH HOPE OF RESURRECTION

1. We shall go out with hope of re-sur-rec - tion,__ we shall go out, from strength to strength go on,__ we shall go out and__ tell our sto-ries bold - ly,__ tales of a love__ that will not let us go.__ We'll sing our

Words: © 1993 June Boyce-Tillman.
Stainer & Bell Ltd and Women in Theology. From *Reflecting Praise*
Music: *Londonderry Air* (Irish traditional melody)

songs of wrongs that can be right - ed,_____ we'll dream our

dreams of hearts that can be healed,_____ we'll weave a

cloth of all the world u - ni - ted_____ with - in a

vi - sion of a Christ that sets us free._____

1. We shall go out with hope of resurrection,
   we shall go out, from strength to strength go on,
   we shall go out and tell our stories boldly,
   tales of a love that will not let us go.
   We'll sing our songs of wrongs that can be righted,
   we'll dream our dreams of hearts that can be healed,
   we'll weave a cloth of all the world united
   within a vision of a Christ that sets us free.

2. We'll give a voice to those who have not spoken,
   we'll find the words for those whose lips are sealed.
   We'll make the tunes for those who sing no longer,
   vibrating love alive in every heart.
   We'll shout for joy with those who still are weeping,
   chant hymns of strength for hearts that break in grief.
   We'll leap and dance the resurrection story,
   including all within the circles of our love.

See also material from Section 6, *Women*

# ACKNOWLEDGEMENTS

The editors and publishers would like to thank all those who have granted permission for the use of material in this book. Every effort has been made to trace and identify copyright holders and to secure necessary permission for reprinting. If we have erred in any respect, we apologize and would be glad to make any necessary amendments in subsequent editions of this book.

### Environment and Land

p. 4    'O Lord, O God', from An African Prayer Book, ed. Desmond Tutu, © Hodder and Stoughton, 1995.

p. 5    'In the beginning', © Miriam Therese Winter, from Woman Prayer, Woman Song, Meyer Stone Books. Used with permission of The Crossroad Publishing Company and HarperCollinsReligious, Australia.

p. 6    'Ripped from the land?' © Chico Buarque, from Terra: Struggle of the Landless, Sebastiao Salgado, Phaidon Press, 1997.

p. 7    'If the land could speak', Kalinga tribal people, Philippines. 'Pilgrim God', © Annabel Shilson-Thomas.

p. 8    'Stop destroying the forest', The Penang people of Sarawak, Malaysia, from Survival International.

p. 9    'At the heart of everything is land', Aboriginal people, Australia. 'Lord God, creator of all the earth', Filipino tribal prayer from Looking at The Philippines Through the Eyes of the Poor, © Vin McMullen/CAFOD, 1992. 'So long as ... I shall sing no celebratory song', © Cecil Rajendra, from Refugees and Other Despairs, Choice Books, Singapore.

p. 11    'And the smog', © Prof. E. Just, from LifeStyle Newsletter.

p. 12    'We in the Third World', Bernard Guri, Ghanaian agriculturalist. 'To plant a tree', © Rev. Francis Simons, from God is Green, Ian Bradley, Darton, Longman and Todd, 1990.

p. 13    'Every part of this shining earth is sacred', based on Chief Seattle's Testimony.

p. 14    'Recognizing that the earth ... ', Shakertown pledge.

## Basic Needs

p. 30    'It is not enough to conquer hunger', Pope Paul VI. 'I was homeless, but you said to me', © Anton Iniguez from CAFOD Campaign, *Proclaim Jubilee*, CAFOD, 1987.

p. 31    'Forgive us, Lord our God', © Sheila Cassidy, from *Triumph of Hope*, CAFOD, 1996.

p. 32    'With the people of — ', © Annabel Shilson-Thomas.

p. 34    'O mighty and merciful God', from *Morning Noon and Night: Prayers and Meditations from the Third World*, ed. John Carden, © Church Missionary Society, 1976.

p. 35    'Apollo 2 cost more than Apollo 1', © Leonel Rugama, Nicaraguan Ministry of Culture, 1986, from *Continent of Hope*, CAFOD.

p. 37    'My name is Gary', Gary Gallard, © ATD Fourth World, from *Fourth World Journal*, autumn 1995. 'Holy God, as you plucked up the people of Israel', © Annabel Shilson-Thomas.

p. 38    'When we rise each morning', Martin Luther King Jr. 'Lord of Creation', taken from *Good Friday People* by Sheila Cassidy, published and copyright 1991 by Darton, Longman and Todd Ltd and used by kind permission of the publishers.

p. 39    'All the broken hearts', © Sun Ai Lee from the poem 'Prophesy', first published in the journal *In God's Image*, April 1986 (Hong Kong).

## The Excluded

p. 50    'O God, oh why aren't we heard with our voices', © Seamus Neville/ADT Fourth World, from *Fourth World Journal*, winter 1995/96. 'We can turn away', Andrew Sinyavskycou, from *Torture: a Cancer in our Society*, Catholic Institute for International Relations (CIIR).

p. 51    'Creator God, open our eyes', Jimmy Palso (adapted), South Africa. 'Lord, you entered Jerusalem to cheers of "Hosanna!"' © Annabel Shilson-Thomas.

p. 53    'went to an all black school', © Michael Smith from *Heinneman Book of Caribbean Poetry*, 1992.

p. 54    'Before the fear of HIV/AIDS', © CAFOD, from CAFOD World AIDS Day, 1993.

p. 55    'You may be in another country', Bartholomew Bo Deng, Kakuma Camp, Sudan.

p. 56    'Used, abused and throwaway', Shay Cullen, © Columban Fathers, Far East, March 1996.

p. 57    'I pray for the ones who help me', Mana from Ethiopia. 'The *guerrillero* came down from the mountain', © Bill Lewis from *Christian: Living for a Change*, Nov/Dec 1987.

p. 58    'You ask me, what did I dream?' 14-year-old Vietnamese boy, from *Borders and Barriers*, © Uniya/Jesuit Refugee Service, Sydney, Australia.

p. 60    'Lord, we confess our day to day failure', from the Cathedral Church of St George, Cape Town, South Africa.

## Conflict, War and Peace

p. 72    'Lord, my country bleeds', Chris Eddy, from *Prayer Handbook*, © The Methodist Church. 'God of all ages and peoples', from *Frontliner*, reproduced in Philippines Ecumenical Network (PEN) Newsletter Number 10.

p. 74    'O, the despair that wells up in me', a Crisis Monitor, from *Meditations on the Natal Violence*, PACSA (Pietermaritzburg Agency for Christian Social Awareness), South Africa, June 1990.

p. 75    'How wonderful it is, how pleasant', Zephania Kaneeta, from *Why O Lord: Psalms and Sermons from Namibia*, © World Council of Churches, Geneva, Switzerland, 1986. 'Standing guard without supplies', Rebecca Larsen, from *What is you Church doing about Landmines?* © World Council of Churches, Geneva, Switzerland, 1996.

p. 76    'Our Father, who art in Heaven', refugees from El Salvador, from *Working in Partnership: Central America Prayer and Liturgies*, © CAFOD.

p. 77    'I have not yet reached the shore', reproduced from Amnesty International poster in *Let my people go*, © Michael Evans, Kevin Mayhew Ltd, 1976.

p. 78    'if i chant a poem', © Bill Lewis from 'Communion', *Christian: Living for a Change*.

p. 79    'gentle breeze and piercing cold', Ludy Panaligan, from *SAMIN News*, © Good Shepherd Sisters Association in Mindanao.

p. 81    'For the caged bird', Violetta Parra from *Changemakers 2000 Latin America Focus*, CAFOD/Christian Aid.

p. 82    'Blessed Bakhita, we rejoice', Archbishop of Sudan.

p. 83    'I dream of a community', Clementina Naita, Lodwar Youth Programme, Kenya, from *They shall not rob us of hope*, CAFOD, 1995.

## Work and Debt

p. 94    'I used to think when I was a child', Helder Camara, Brazil. 'The rich industrialist from the North', source unknown, Asia.

p. 95    'Don't seize control', © Janet Morley, from *Who Runs the World? Ideas for Worship Leaders*, Christian Aid, 1994.

p. 97    'Lord, the motor under me is running hot', from *An African Prayer Book*, ed. Desmond Tutu, Hodder and Stoughton, 1995.

p. 98    'You are the God of the poor', Misa Campesina de Nicaragua, from *Continent of Hope*, CAFOD. 'Come, come and let us listen to the stories', Filipino song, © Fabella/Lee/Suh, Orbis Books, from *Asian Christian Spirituality*, 1992.

p. 99    'We raise the wheat', slave song, 1855. 'Perhaps if the churches had had the courage', © Dorothy Sayers, from *Unpopular Opinions*, Victor Gollancz, 1946.

p. 100    'You are the God of the poor, the God at work in the factory', © *Worship and Prayers from and for Central America*. Publishers unknown.

p. 101    'We pray for world leaders', © Linda Jones.

p. 102    'We firmly believe, Lord', Latin America

p. 103    'Time in Asia', © Kosuke Koyama, from *No Handle on the Cross*, Orbis Books, 1977.

p. 104    'When the tourists flew in', © Cecil Rajendra.

p. 105    'For the times when we have taken other people's work for granted', © Linda Jones.

p. 106    'A multinational', Helder Camara, from *Hoping Against All Hope*, © Orbis Books, 1984.

## Women

p. 118    'Woman of Africa', © Okot p'Bitck, from *People and Progress*, BBC/Save the Children. 'With Miriam, who with Moses and Aaron', B.D'Arcy, from *The Trampled Vineyard*, © CHAS/UNLEASH (The Catholic Housing Aid Society/United London Ecumenical Action on Single Homelessness), 1992.

p. 119    'I am a woman' © Elizabeth Tapia, from *Women Hold up Half the Sky*, CAFOD/Christian Aid.

p. 120    'She is the Madonna of the Plains', © Patricia Mack, Australia.

p. 121    'I saw you in the doorway', © M.T.Winter, Medical Mission Sisters, from *Women Witness*, 1992. Used with the permission of the Crossroad Publishing Company.

p. 123    'Daughters of Jerusalem', © Janet Morley, from *Bread of Tomorrow*, ed. Janet Morley, SPCK/Christian Aid, 1992.

p. 124    'Sister and brother workers!' Asian Women Workers, from *CAW*, Vol.2, No.4, December 1983.

p. 125    'I believe in God, our mother all powerful', Pastoral Andina, Peru.

p. 126    'Your feet tell the toll', Africa.

## Solidarity

p. 136  'You asked for my hands', © Joe Seremane, from *Lifelines*, ed. Pamela Searle, Christian Aid, 1987.

p. 137  'An Ancient Rabbi once asked', ancient Jewish story from *Were you there?* Rosemary Hartill, SPCK, 1995. 'We talk of "living in Christ with people"', reproduced from *Oceans of Prayer*, 1991, with the permission of the National Christian Educational Council.

p. 138  'Don't moralize', Moraene Roberts, from *Fourth World*, summer 1995, © ATD Fourth World.

p. 139  'Lord, is it not possible . . .', © Fermin Cebolla Lopez from *Prayers of the New Man*, publisher unknown. 'On the night before his death', Gerard Hughes from *Triumph of Hope*, CAFOD, 1996.

p. 140  'Come, Lord, do not smile and say you are already with us', Helder Camara, from *The Desert is Fertile*. © Orbis Books, 1974.

p. 141  'We shall have to repent in this generation', Martin Luther King. 'Compassionate God', © Annabel Shilson-Thomas. 'My God, I need to have signs of your grace', © Rubem Alves, Brazil.

p. 142  'Lord of all creation', © The Association of Rabbis of the Reform Synagogue of Great Britain, from *Transcendence*, Westminster Interfaith.

p. 143  'Our God who art in heaven', © Linda Jones.

p. 144  'God our guide', Alain Rocourt, reproduced from *Oceans of Prayer*, with the permission of the National Christian Education Council, 1991.

p. 145  'I believe in the equality of all', Ayacucho Youth group, Peru, Comision Episcopal de Accion Social, Lima, Peru. 'God help us to change,' © Collins/Leuing, from *A Common Prayer*, Collins-Dove, 1990.

## Celebrating Hope

p. 156  'Creator God, we announce your goodness', The Masai, Kenya.

p. 157  'O God of all youth, we pray to you', Brazil youth group. 'Stand up and look at the mountain', Victor Jara, Chile.

p. 158  'When the heart is hard and parched up', © Rabindranath Tagore, from *Gitanjali*, Macmillan Publishers, 1971. 'I am a youth', Uwimana Uwamaholo Le Kheng, Rwanda, 1995.

p. 160  'I'm my mother's eldest son', Domingo Claudio, from *Encounters Lost Children of Angola*, produced by Barraclough Carey for Channel Four Television Company, Ltd.

p. 161  'I, sinner and bishop', Pedro Casaldaligo, from *Continent of Hope*, CAFOD.

p. 162  'O God, our loving and Eternal Parent', from *An African Prayer Book*, ed. Desmond Tutu, © Hodder and Stoughton, 1995.

p. 163  'Our Father who is in us here on earth', Central American Lord's Prayer (shortened) from *Dare to Dream*, ed. Geoffrey Duncan, Fount, HarperCollins, 1995.

p. 164  'How lonely I am in the unknown world', a South African migrant worker, from *Refugees*, liturgical booklet, CAFOD. 'God who listens and hears when we pray', © Linda Jones.

p. 165  'Our culture has taught', Miriam Rose Ungunmerr, from *The Aboriginal Gift*, publisher unknown.

p. 166  'Live slowly, think slowly, for time is a mystery', © Ben Okri, from 'Benediction to an English Friend in Africa', *An African Elegy*, Jonathan Cape.

# TYPE INDEX

## *Prayers*

## Readings

## Sayings

### BASIC NEEDS
When a man's stomach, 36

### SOLIDARITY
We cannot know, 139
When spiders unite, 138

## Songs

### ENVIRONMENT AND LAND
All praise to you, 16
God, beyond all names, 20
God bless the grass, 66
Many and great, 18
Think of a world, 24

### BASIC NEEDS
Christ, be our light, 40
Here in the busy city, 44
Think of a world, 24
When I needed a neighbour, 43

### THE EXCLUDED
A touching place, 64
Christ, be our light, 40
God bless the grass, 66
Jesus Christ is waiting, 62
Siph' amandla, 107
When I needed a neighbour, 43

### CONFLICT, WAR AND PEACE
Dona nobis pacem, 88
La paz del Señor, 86
Lord, while the world with war and hatred
    burns, 84
The peace of God, 89

### WORK AND DEBT
If you believe and I believe, 108
It's no life, 110
Lord, you have come to the seashore, 112
Siph' amandla, 107

### WOMEN
Enemy of apathy, 130
God bless the grass, 66
Stand, O stand firm, 127
We shall go out with hope of resurrection,
    177
Women speak justice, 128

### SOLIDARITY
A touching place, 64
Christ, be our light, 40
If you believe and I believe, 108
Jesu, Jesu, fill us with your love, 148
Jesus Christ is waiting, 62
Sent by the Lord am I, 150
The servant song, 146
When I needed a neighbour, 43
Who will speak, 152

### CELEBRATING HOPE
City of God, 170
Gloria, gloria, 167
God, beyond all names, 20
Siyahamba, 168
We have hope, 174
We shall go out with hope of resurrection,
    177

# THEMATIC INDEX

## Environment and Land

## Basic Needs

## The Excluded

Come, come and let us listen to the
  stories, 98
Creator God, open our eyes, 51
gentle breeze and piercing cold, 79
God bless the grass, 66
Holy God, as you plucked up the people of
  Israel, 37
How wonderful it is, how pleasant, 75
I am a youth, 158
I'm my mother's eldest son, 160
I pray for the ones who help me, 57
I saw you in the doorway, 121
I was homeless, but you said to me, 30
In Christ there is neither Jew nor Greek, 58
Is not this the fast that I choose ...?, 36
Jesus Christ is waiting, 62
Lord, you entered Jerusalem to cheers of
  'Hosanna!', 51
Lord, we confess, 60
My name is Gary, 37
O mighty and merciful God, 34
O, the despair that wells up in me!, 74
Oh God, oh why aren't we heard with our
  voices?, 50
Our God, who art in heaven, 143
Pilgrim God, 7
Ripped from the land?, 6
Siph' amandla, 107
The guerrillero came down from the
  mountain, 57
The Lord is near to the broken-hearted, 49
Then the righteous will answer him ..., 35
Used, abused and throwaway, 56
We can turn away and avoid seeing, 50
We raise the wheat, 99
We talk of 'living in Christ with people', 137
went to an all black school, 53
When I needed a neighbour, 43
With the people of —, we remember, 32
Women speak justice, 128
You are the God of the poor, 98
You ask me, what did I dream?, 58
You may be in another country, 55

## Conflict, War and Peace
Blessed are the peacemakers, 71
Blessed Bakhita, we rejoice, 82
By the tender mercy of our God, 83
Death has come up into our windows, 73
Dona nobis pacem, 88
For the caged bird, 81
gentle breeze and piercing cold, 79
God of all ages and peoples, 72
Holy God, as you plucked up the people of
  Israel, 37
How wonderful it is, how pleasant, 75
I am a youth, 158

I'm my mother's eldest son, 160
I dream of a community, 83
I have not yet reached the shore, 77
if I chant a poem, 78
If the land could speak, 7
La paz del Señor, 86
Lord, my country bleeds, 72
Lord, we confess, 60
Lord, while the world with war and hatred
  burns, 84
O, the despair that wells up in me!, 74
Our Father who art in heaven, 76
Ripped from the land?, 6
Standing guard without supplies, 75
Stop destroying the forest, 8
The peace of God, 89
The wolf shall dwell with the lamb, 161
We can turn away and avoid seeing, 50
With the people of —, we remember, 32
You ask me, what did I dream?, 58
You may be in another country, 55

## Work and Debt
A multinational, 106
And the smog, 11
Apollo 2 cost more than Apollo 1, 35
Come, come and let us listen to the
  stories, 98
Come to me all who labour, 93
Don't seize control, 95
For the times when we have taken, 105
Here in the busy city, 44
How lonely I am, 164
I am a woman, 119
I used to think when I was a child, 94
If the land could speak, 7
If you believe and I believe, 108
It's no life, 110
Land will not be sold absolutely, 9
Lord, my country bleeds, 72
Lord, the motor under me is running hot, 97
Lord, you have come to the sea-shore, 112
Our God, who art in heaven, 143
Perhaps if the churches, 99
Siph' amandla, 107
Sister and brother workers, 124
So long as ... I shall sing no celebratory
  song, 9
Stop destroying the forest, 8
The rich industrialist from the North, 95
Time in Asia, 103
We firmly believe, Lord, 102
We in the Third World, 12
We pray for world leaders, 101
We raise the wheat, 99
When the tourists flew in, 104
When we rise each morning, 38

189  THEMATIC INDEX